Ce
Do
St

THE SAS AND SPECIAL FORCES GUIDE TO

Escape and Evasion

THE SAS AND SPECIAL FORCES GUIDE TO

Escape and Evasion

WILL FOWLER

SPELLMOUNT

Staplehurst

British Library Cataloguing in Publication Data:
A catalogue record for this book is available
from the British Library

Copyright © Amber Books Ltd 2005

ISBN 1-86227-277-8

First published in the UK in 2005 by
SPELLMOUNT LTD
The Village Centre
Staplehurst
Kent TN12 0BJ

Tel: 01580 893730
Fax: 01580 893731
e-mail: enquiries@spellmount.com
Website: www.spellmount.com

Editorial and design by
Amber Books Ltd
Bradley's Close
74-77 White Lion Street
London N1 9PF
www.amberbooks.co.uk

Project Editor: Michael Spilling
Copy Editor: Chris McNab
Design: Zoë Mellors
Picture Research: Natasha Jones

Printed in Italy

CONTENTS

CHAPTER 1

Introduction

Happily, few of us will ever eject from a crippled combat aircraft, or be cut off on a battlefield after a firefight and find ourselves on the run from hostile forces intent on killing or capturing us and then parading us as religious or class enemies on international television.

We are unlikely to be captured, manacled, interrogated and assaulted and then locked up. However, throughout the world ordinary men, women and even children have been caught up in tribal, religious or ethnic conflicts and found themselves in such grim predicaments. Military personnel are more obviously vulnerable.

The male or female soldier or pilot goes into action with a range of equipment to help him or her survive alone or as part of a small group. He will carry the tools of survival: lightweight rations, signalling and communications equipment, first aid packs and fishing and hunting kits. (For the purposes of simplicity in this handbook, the evading pilot or soldier will be referred to as 'he'.) However, it is not just the 'prone to capture' pilot or special forces soldier who could find himself in the role of unwelcome guest behind enemy lines, being hotly pursued by a hunter-killer force. Once the shooting starts, it could happen at any time to any military personnel.

The 'rescue at any cost' philosophy that characterized USAF and US Navy operations in South East Asia, and those of NATO in the Balkans and the Middle East conflicts, may not be possible in the future. Friendly military forces trapped behind enemy lines in future conflicts may not experience quick recovery. Soldiers may have to move for extended times and over long distances to reach places less threatening to the recovery forces. The soldier may not know the type of recovery to expect – each situation and the available resources determine the type of recovery possible. What is important is that the soldier is able to construct a meaningful plan of escape, evasion and survival without any external assistance.

Opposite: Amid a background of signal flares, soldiers participate in a night-time training exercise. In the noise and confusion of a night-time firefight, a soldier may lose contact with his unit or be wounded and taken prisoner.

7

THE SURVIVAL PLAN

The basis for escape and evasion can be summed up by the acronym SURVIVAL. A soldier in an E&E situation should:

S – Size Up...

Size Up the Situation. If he is in a combat situation, the soldier should find a place where he can conceal himself from the enemy. Remember, security takes priority. He should use his senses of hearing, smell and sight to get a feel for the battlefield. What is the enemy doing? Advancing? Holding in place? Retreating? He will have to consider battlefield developments when he makes his escape and survival plan.

Size Up the Surroundings. He should determine the pattern of the area and get a feel for what is going on around him. Every environment, whether forest, jungle or desert, has a rhythm or pattern. This rhythm or pattern includes animal, insect and bird noises and activity. It may also include enemy and civilian movements.

Size Up Physical Condition. The pressure of the recent combat or the trauma of being in a survival situation may have caused him to overlook wounds he has received. He must check himself for injuries and give first aid while taking care to prevent further bodily harm. For instance, in any climate, he must drink plenty of water to prevent dehydration.

Size Up Equipment. Perhaps in the heat of battle, he has lost or damaged some of his equipment. The soldier checks to see what equipment he has and its condition.

Below: During survival, evasion, resistance and escape (SERE) training, a US Special Forces soldier checks his ALICE pack that contains many key long-term survival tools; others, like his compass and combat knife, will be on his person.

TYPICAL MILITARY ESCAPE AND EVASION SITUATIONS

- A unit may have been decimated after being surrounded by the enemy, but some men have managed to escape.
- The enemy has overrun a defensive position, but there are survivors who must get away before the enemy returns to start mopping-up.
- A soldier has broken out from a PoW holding area behind the battlefield.
- A patrol has become lost behind enemy lines.
- A soldier has accidentally strayed through the enemy frontline.
- A soldier has managed to escape from a PoW camp further into occupied territory.
- While on a peace-keeping mission, a unit is ambushed and all but a few have been captured.

U – Use All Senses, Undue Haste Makes Waste

The soldier may make a wrong move if he reacts quickly without thinking or planning. That move may result in his capture or death. The rule is – don't move just for the sake of taking action. He should consider all aspects of the situation before he makes a decision. If he acts in haste, he may forget or lose some of his equipment. In his haste, he may also become disoriented and find himself lost. The trained soldier plans his moves and is ready to move out quickly when the safe opportunity arises. He uses all his senses to evaluate the situation and is continually observant. It is important that he stay calm while attempting to evade captors, for it is easy to panic. Carefully thinking through a course of action will pay great dividends. The US Air Force pilot Captain Scott O'Grady successfully evaded Serbian troops for six days in war-torn Bosnia. His commander noted that O'Grady's ability to 'maintain his cool' played a key role in this achievement. O'Grady moved slowly and carefully while avoiding hostile troops, never venturing more than 3.2km (2 miles) from the spot where he initially landed.

R – Remember Your Location

The soldier should find his location on a map and relate it to the surrounding terrain. This is a basic principle that he must always follow. If there are other persons with him, he makes sure they also know their location. He should also find out who in the group has a map and compass. If that person is killed, he will have to get these items from him. The soldier must pay close attention to where he is going, not relying on others in the group to keep track of the route. He must constantly orient himself and always try to determine how his location relates to –

- The location of enemy units and controlled areas.
- The location of friendly units and controlled areas.
- The location of local water sources (especially important in the desert).
- Areas that will provide good cover and concealment.

V – Vanquish Fear and Panic

The greatest enemies in a combat survival and evasion situation are fear and panic. They can destroy the soldier's ability to make an intelligent decision and may cause him to react to his feelings and imagination rather than to his situation. They can drain his energy and thereby promote negative emotions. Previous survival and evasion training and self-confidence will enable him to vanquish fear and panic.

I – Improvise

Most of the citizens of the United States and western Europe have tools, clothing and food readily available. Many of these items are cheap to replace when damaged. This easy-come, easy-go, easy-to-replace culture makes it unnecessary for civilians to improvise. Such inexperience is an enemy in a survival situation.

Escape and evasion training teaches a soldier how to improvise. He should take a tool designed for a specific purpose and see how many other uses he can put it to, and he should never pass by anything that could be of value. A discarded bin liner or a plastic fertilizer bag can make an emergency waterproof over-garment. An abandoned steel helmet, not too common in these days of composites, makes a good cooking pot or water carrier, but he should look out for any metal container that will do these jobs. Natural objects can be applied to different needs. An example is using a rock for a hammer. No matter how complete a survival kit he has, it will run out or wear out after a while. The soldier's imagination must take over when professional kit is absent.

V – Value Living

Everyone is born kicking and fighting to live, but many people are used to the soft life and become creatures of comfort. What happens when we are faced with a survival situation with its stresses, inconveniences and discomforts? This is when the will to live – placing a high value on living – is vital. The experience and knowledge gained through life and military training will have a bearing on the soldier's will to live. Stubbornness, and a refusal to give in to problems and obstacles, will give him the mental and physical strength to endure.

A – Act Like the Natives

The natives and animals of a region have adapted to their environment. To get a feel for the area, the soldier watches how the people go about their daily routine.
• When and what do they eat?
• When, where and how do they get their food?
• When and where do they go for water?
• What time do they usually go to bed and get up?
Observing such routines are important when trying to avoid capture. In a friendly area, the soldier could build a rapport with the natives by showing interest in their

tools and how they get food and water. By studying the people, he can learn to respect them, make valuable friends and, most importantly, learn how to adapt to their environment and increase his chances of survival.

Animals in the area can also provide clues on how to survive. Like humans, they require food, water and shelter. By watching them, the soldier can find sources of water and food (remembering that not all animal foods are edible for humans). He should keep in mind, however, that the reaction of animals – birds flying away or curious cows wandering towards him – can reveal his presence to the enemy.

L – Live by Wits (but for now) Learn Basic Skills

Without training in basic skills for surviving and evading on the battlefield, the soldier's chances of living through a combat survival and evasion situation are slight.

He should learn these basic skills well before he heads into combat. How he decides to equip himself before deployment will impact on whether or not he will survive. He needs to know about the environment to which he is going, and must practice basic skills geared to that environment. For instance, if he is headed for a desert, he needs to know how to get water. He should practice basic survival skills during all training programs and exercises. Survival training reduces fear of the unknown and gives self-confidence. It teaches him to live by his wits.

Many of the techniques and skills that have been developed and refined for the military have a wider application for civilian walkers, lightweight campers and wildlife enthusiasts. Even the general reader will measure himself against the advice in this book and wonder, 'Could I escape, evade and survive?'

Below: A US Marine crawls through mud on an obstacle course at the Fort Sherman Jungle Operations Training Center. Often the least comfortable route or location is the safest in a survival and evasion situation.

CHAPTER 2

Evading Capture

When planning for an operation, a soldier or pilot must consider how, if disaster strikes, he will avoid capture and return to his unit. Prior planning and sound evasion technique will help him to stay one step ahead of his pursuers.

Contingency plans must be prepared in conjunction with unit Standing Operating Procedures (SOPs). Intelligence sections can help prepare personnel for contingency actions through information supplied in area studies, SERE (survival, evasion, resistance and escape) contingency guides, threat briefings, current intelligence reports and current contact and authentication procedures. Pre-mission preparation includes the completion of a Contingency Plan of Action, or CPA document. The study and research needed to develop the CPA will make the soldier or pilot aware of the current situation in his mission area. His CPA will let recovery forces know his probable actions if he has to move to avoid capture. He should start preparing even before pre-mission planning. Many parts of the CPA will be SOP for his unit and should be included in his training.

The CPA is his entire plan for his return to friendly control. He should prepare his CPA in three phases. During his normal training, he prepares paragraph 1 – Situation Planning. During his pre-mission planning, he prepares paragraphs 2 – Mission, 3 – Execution, 4 – Command, and 5 – Communications. After deployment into an area, he continually updates his CPA, based on mission changes and intelligence updates. The CPA is a guide. He may add or delete certain

Opposite: Using a mixture of man-made and natural camouflage materials, a sniper breaks up the outline of his head. The soft brim of the jungle hat shields his eyes, but unlike a helmet does not present a straight line.

portions based on the mission. The CPA may be a recovery force's only means of determining his location and intentions after he starts to move. It is an essential tool for the soldier or pilot's survival and return to friendly control.

He can take most of the Situation planning paragraph in the operation order format with him on the mission. Paragraph 1 will cover his unit's assigned area and potential mission areas of the world. It may come from open or closed sources, but will contain the information he needs to complete a CPA. Pilots will have greater access to open sources, which may include newspapers, magazines, country or area handbooks, area studies, television, radio and persons familiar with the area. Closed sources may include area studies, area assessments, SERE contingency guides, various classified field manuals and intelligence reports.

STANDING OPERATING PROCEDURES

Unit Standing Operating Procedures (SOPs) – pre-defined procedures for military operations – are valuable tools that will help a soldier's operational planning. When faced with a dangerous situation requiring immediate action, it is not the time to discuss options; it is the time to act. Many of the techniques used during small unit

movement can be carried over to fit requirements for moving and returning to friendly control. The SOPs should include, but are not limited to –

Movement team size

The larger the evading group, the easier it will be to track down. If possible, the group should try and break down into pairs, as this could split up the tracking team or even leave them all tracking just one trail. In most situations, two heads are better than one and when rest becomes a necessity, one soldier can remain on guard while the other sleeps.

Team communications (technical and non-technical)

This can include hand signals as well as combat net radios.

Essential equipment

There are three different types of loads: fighting, mission and existence. The soldier decides what items will make up these loads, where they are carried, and what will be done with them upon contact with the enemy.

1) The fighting load consists of those items of equipment, weapons, ammunition, food and water that are common to all soldiers and are necessary for immediate

Above: This photograph shows the range of equipment carried by a British soldier in his personal load carrying equipment (PLCE), and includes ammunition magazines, cleaning kit, maps, prismatic compass, mess tins, first aid kit, survival kit, cooker and rations.

use in combat or survival. These items are normally carried on the person and are retained at all times while in contact with the enemy.

2) The mission load consists of those items of equipment or ammunition that are required by the mission but are not normally carried by all soldiers in a unit. The load may include spare batteries, demolitions, radios, anti-tank weapons or mines. This load is normally spread out among members of the unit and is rotated often. It may be dropped upon enemy contact, but is normally carried to the objective and either used or emplaced there.

3) The existence load consists of any items designed to provide protection from the elements: sleeping gear, changes of clothes, spare rations or tentage. This load may or may not be brought into the objective area, depending on the tactical situation. If it is brought, it is normally dropped upon enemy contact or left in an assembly area and retrieved later.

Maps are important. Before a mission, the soldier should make a simple map on a sheet of paper from a waterproof notepad. It should show just the basic routes, roads, rivers and major topographical features. The map should be sewn or concealed in his uniform. If captured, while awaiting escape, the soldier can make a rudimentary map by drawing on the inside of his clothing, as this will greatly aid his post-escape navigation plans. Once on the run, he should acquire a better map by searching bodies and deserted buildings and, particularly in an urban environment, look inside vehicles or even check out phone boxes.

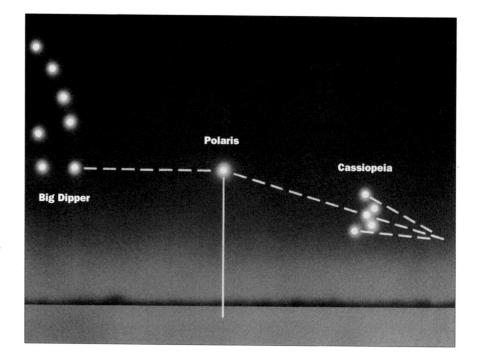

Right: The Pole (North) Star is a true guide to north, and is set between the Big Dipper (Plough) and Cassiopeia. To locate the Pole Star, use the Big Dipper by drawing an imaginary line through the constellation (as here).

NAVIGATION WITHOUT A COMPASS

The sensible soldier will always carry a mini compass in his survival kit, plus one hidden in his clothing. This is one of the most treasured items of Escape and Evasion kit. He can also make an emergency compass by magnetizing a needle and sitting it on a free-floating leaf on water.

If the soldier becomes a survivor/ evader and does not have a compass, he can use the stars at night to find north. The North Star is at the very end of the handle of a cluster of stars known in the United States as the Little Dipper. It can also be located by using the Big Dipper, or Plough as it is known in the UK. Measure the distance between the two stars that form the end of the 'pan' or front on the plough. Follow a straight line through those two stars and measure along that line five times the thickness of the pan to locate the North or Pole Star. If the survivor/evader is close to 30° latitude, the North Star should be three hand widths above the horizon. The farther north he

Above: The Southern Cross is the most distinctive constellation in the Southern Hemisphere. The Coalsack, a dark nebula, is to the southeast of the Southern Cross.

travels, the higher it will be in the sky. On the North Pole, it would be almost overhead. Near the Equator, it is invisible, and its approximate location must be found by looking for the Big Dipper or Cassiopeia.

In the Southern Hemisphere, the survivor/ evader can find due south by looking for the Southern Cross. It rotates around the South Pole. If a line is drawn from the top of the cross straight through the bottom and on across the sky, the line will pass through a due south point. At about -30° latitude, the imaginary 'South Star' will be about three hand widths above the horizon. There is no southern pole star.

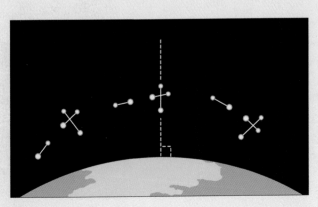

Left: When the Southern Cross appears upright in the night sky (ie, with its long axis vertical), a line taken vertically down to the horizon indicates geographic south.

ESCAPE MAPS

Silk escape maps are now a standard part of a pilot's survival equipment. Cloth map invention is credited to Christopher Clayton Hutton. Hutton worked for MI9, a subsection of British Military Intelligence during World War II. Hutton was tasked by the War Office to create the escape gear for British servicemen.

Hutton secretly met with the map publisher John Bartholomew in 1940. Bartholomew supplied maps to Hutton covering Germany, France, Poland, Italy, Austria, Switzerland, Belgium, Holland and the Balkans. Bartholomew waived all copyrights to the map data in support of the war effort. After Hutton got the cartographic source, he needed a medium onto which he could print the maps. The maps needed to be quiet to unfold and easy to conceal, safe from disintegration when wet, and also had to maintain their integrity when folded at the crease line. After many attempts to print on silk squares, he was about to give up. Then he thought of adding Pectin, a form of wax, to the ink so that it would not run or wash out when submerged, even in seawater.

Hutton printed escape maps on silk, man-made fibre and tissue paper. The tissue paper was very special, in that it was not made from wood pulp like conventional paper, but from Mulberry leaves. This hybrid paper had the texture of onion skin and extreme durability. The tissue paper could be crumpled and soaked, and then flattened out without creases. All the integrity of a new map was there, no data faded or disintegrated and it could folded up in such a fashion that it would occupy a very small space, such as inside a chess piece. In November 1942, a small contingent of American Intelligence Officers came to Britain to learn of British escape and evasion techniques. Each officer received a leather-bound copy of a book called Per Ardua Libertas. In this book, there were examples of each cloth or tissue escape maps that had been produced to date. After this meeting with the British, the United States began to produce its own escape maps.

Actions at danger areas

The lead scout may advance while the remainder of the group remain well spaced out of the danger area, until the point man has signalled that the area is safe.

Signalling techniques

Hand signals are silent and allow instructions or information to be passed quickly between people who may be many metres apart. Though there are widely used signals in rehearsals, some may be invented that are specific to the mission.

Immediate action drills

If the group is ambushed, it immediately counterattacks the ambush party, and attempts to fight through or execute a fighting retreat.

HELICOPTER RECOVERY DEVICES AND PROCEDURES

The group will need to know the type of helicopter and its capacity. Is it a large troop carrier or a small liaison aircraft? Is it a two-door or single-door aircraft and where are the danger areas in relation to the tail rotor? If working in jungle, it may be necessary to use a winch.

Security procedures during movement and at hide sites

Hides need to be approached using routes that will not become trodden down to create obvious tracks. This may mean using rocky ground or dense vegetation. If paths are trodden down, they should fit into the contours of the terrain – for example, around the edge of a field and not diagonally across it.

Rally points or rendezvous (RV)

If the group is 'bumped' by an enemy patrol, the drill may be to 'bomb burst' or scatter in all directions and return to regroup at the last RV.

Link-up procedures

These may be part of the RV procedure – RVs will be identified by the group leader as the patrol or operation progresses, or may have been identified during the briefing.

Below: A US Army special forces vehicle maintains security as a UH-60 Black Hawk helicopter lifts off from a rendezvous point in southern Afghanistan, June 2004. Special forces rely heavily on helicopter recovery to carry out operations.

Rehearsals work effectively for reinforcing these SOP skills and also provide opportunities for evaluation and improvement. The group leader should be able to assess some of the likely obstacles or situations that may be encountered and brief his team so that SOPs can be rehearsed.

Right: A team from the US Army's 1st Infantry Division searches the terrain for hostile activity during a Quick Response Force (QRF) mission on June 19, 2004, central Iraq. A QRF would be called out to conduct a sweep if the presence of an escaper and evader had been established.

NOTIFICATION TO MOVE AND AVOID CAPTURE

An isolated unit has several general courses of action it can take to avoid the capture of the group or its individuals. However, these courses of action do not replace the original mission. A commander cannot arbitrarily abandon the assigned mission. Rather, he may adopt these courses of action after completing his mission, when his unit cannot complete its assigned objective (because of combat power losses) or when he receives orders to extract his unit from its current position.

The commander may decide to have the unit move to avoid capture and return to friendly control. In this case, as long as there is communication with higher headquarters, that headquarters will make the decision. If the unit commander loses contact with higher headquarters, he must make the decision to move or wait. He bases his decision on many factors, including the mission, available rations and ammunition, casualties, the chance of relief by friendly forces and the tactical situation.

Movement team leaders receive their notification through pre-briefed signals.

Once the signal to try to avoid capture is given, it must be passed rapidly to all personnel. The senior officer should notify higher headquarters, if possible. If

Above: At dusk during an escape and evasion exercise, a US Ranger from the 10th Special Forces Group and a soldier from the 2nd Bn The Princess of Wales's Royal Regiment prepare kit in the Eskdalmuir Forest in Scotland.

Above: The Joint Services SERE (Survival, Evasion, Resistance, and Escape) Agency provides training and information for US military personnel and is responsible for the planning and preparation of personnel recovery from combat situations.

unable to communicate with higher headquarters, leaders must recognize that organized resistance has ended, and that centralized organizational control has ceased. Command and control is now at the movement team or individual level and is returned to higher organizational control only after reaching friendly lines.

EXECUTION

Upon notification to avoid capture, all movement team members will try to link up at the initial movement point. This point is where team members rally and actually begin their evasion. They may have tentatively selected the initial movement point during the planning phase through a map reconnaissance. Once on the ground, the team verifies this location or selects a better one. All team members must know its location. The initial movement point should be easy to locate and occupy for a minimum amount of time.

Once the team has rallied at the initial movement point, it must:
• Give first aid.
• Inventory its equipment (decide what to abandon, destroy or retain).
• Apply camouflage.
• Make sure everyone knows the tentative hide locations.
• Ensure everyone knows the primary and alternate routes and rally points en route to the hide locations.
• Always maintain security.
• Split the team into smaller elements. The ideal element should have two to three members; however, it could include more depending on team equipment and experience.

The movement portion of returning to friendly control is the most dangerous, as the survivor/evader is now most vulnerable. It is usually better to move at night because of the concealment darkness offers. Exceptions to such movement would be when he is moving through hazardous terrain or dense vegetation (for example, jungle or mountainous terrain). When moving, he should avoid the following, even if it takes more time and energy to bypass:
• Obstacles and barriers.
• Roads and trails.
• Inhabited areas.
• Waterways and bridges.
• Natural lines of drift.
• Man-made structures.
• All civilian and military personnel.

The best time to travel is at night. However, at night sound carries over very long distances. A rifle shot can be heard at 2.4km (1.5 miles), troop movements at 600m

(1968ft), a rifle being cocked at 500m (1640ft), a man walking through woods at 40m (131ft) and troops digging in at 1000m (3280ft). A cigarette or match can be seen at 800m (2625 feet), a campfire at 6.4km (4 miles), a rifle muzzle flash and a torch or flashlight at 2.4km (1.5 miles). Vehicle headlights can be seen at between 5 and 8km (3 and 5 miles). From the air, these distances can be multiplied two or three times.

BLENDING IN

During an escape and evasion operation, the evader should steer clear of busy or populated areas and keep his distance from any civilians he sees. However, if contact with populated centres is unavoidable, the soldier should:

a) Not act suspiciously or appear to be nervous, as this will attract attention.

b) Never walk in an upright, military fashion – instead he should adopt a tired slouch.

c) Try to at least keep the appearance of being clean and keep shaving if he can.

d) If travelling in countryside, he should carry a spade or some other farming implement.

e) Keep his uniform on underneath any civilian clothing, otherwise he could be shot for being a spy.

f) Keep his watch in a pocket.

g) If approached by the locals, unless he speaks and looks like a native of the area, pretend to be deaf and dumb or perhaps even half-witted.

Above: With camouflage cream smeared across his face and a headover around his neck as protection against the cold, a British soldier scans the terrain before moving off.

PREDICTING THE WEATHER

Rain and wind disguise sounds, and for the evader this can be invaluable. Weather can be predicted during the day by observing cloud patterns while lying up in a hide. By being familiar with the different cloud formations and what weather they portend, the soldier can take action for his protection.

A. CIRRUS CLOUDS

Cirrus clouds are the very high clouds that are actually ice crystals and look like thin streaks or curls. They are usually 6km (3.7 miles) or more above the earth and are typically a sign of fair weather. In cold climates, however, cirrus clouds that begin to multiply, accompanied by increasing winds blowing steadily from the north, indicate an oncoming blizzard.

B. CIRROCUMULUS CLOUDS

Cirrocumulus is a small, white, round cloud at a high altitude. Cirrocumulus clouds indicate good weather.

C. CIRROSTRATUS CLOUDS

Cirrostratus is a fairly uniform layer of high stratus clouds that are darker than cirrus clouds. Cirrostratus clouds indicate good weather.

D. CUMULONIMBUS CLOUDS

Cumulonimbus is the cloud formation resulting from cumulus cloud building up, extending to great heights and forming the shape of an anvil. You can expect a storm if this cloud is moving in your direction.

E. NIMBUS CLOUDS

Nimbus clouds are clouds of uniform greyness that extend over the entire sky. Combined with wind, they can produce rain.

F. CUMULUS CLOUDS

Cumulus clouds are fluffy, white, heaped-up clouds. These clouds, which are much lower than cirrus clouds, often accompany fair weather. They are apt to appear around midday on a sunny day, looking like large cotton balls with flat bottoms. As the day advances, they may become bigger and push higher into the atmosphere. If they pile up to appear like a mountain of clouds. it is an indication of rain squalls.

G. STRATUS CLOUDS

Stratus clouds are very low, grey clouds, often making an even grey layer over the whole sky. These clouds generally mean rain.

H. SCUDS

A loose, vapoury cloud (scud) driven before the wind is a sign of continuing bad weather.

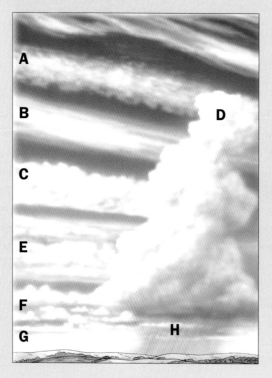

A pilot sees darkness coming up from the ground. It is dark below sooner than it is above – this can be used by a survivor/evader to his advantage. The soldier should take care not to silhouette himself or his movements on the skyline, check to see that his equipment doesn't reflect, or generate noise during rapid movement. Sophisticated thermal-imaging search equipment can detect the heat of a human body in the dark. One ploy is for the soldier to shield his body heat with an aluminium 'space blanket' as a last-ditch effort to escape detection. The body-heat signature will look more like that of a small animal than that generated by a man, as most heat is reflected back by the space blanket.

For night operations, a torch must have a red filter to prevent the user developing an after-image on his retina and it should be attached to the soldier's person or kit by a lanyard. A simple expedient, if a filter is not available, is to paint the bulb with red nail polish. Masking tape can be used to cover the torch glass to produce a pinhead light.

Men have to be closer spaced during travel at night. They must maintain security throughout 360° during movement and at halts. If the group has to

Above: One of the basic lessons of field craft is to avoid silhouetting against open ground, skylines or roads. Here, an evader crosses a road using a culvert as cover: he may keep low and follow the ditch for several yards before emerging.

scatter, it should have a fallback point or RV, perhaps the last stop point or last major landmark or map feature. The survivor/evader should move along, not across, a shadow's line. While going through woods, he should lift his feet high, put the toe down first and test for noise from twigs, leaves and branches, and lower the heel only if there is no obstruction. All clothing must be tight, using rubber bands or insulation tape on trousers to prevent swishing noise in foliage. He should walk about 10 paces and then halt and observe and listen before resuming walking.

Below: At last light, a special forces soldier makes a final check on the route.

TRACKER DOGS

On the run, the survivor/evader will be followed by a hunter force. This may be made up of soldiers or police or a combination of the two. They may have dog teams, which are far more effective than a tracker alone.

The dog follows a trail faster and can continue to track at night. Despite years of domestication, dogs retain most of the traits of their wild ancestors. If put to controlled use, these traits are effective when tracking. A dog can hold a steady pace and effectively track for up to eight hours. The speed is up to around 18km/h (11mph), limited only by the fitness of the handler. Speed and endurance are further increased by the use of vehicles and extra teams. Dogs are curious by nature and can be aggressive or lazy, cowardly or brave. A dog's sensory traits are what make him seem intelligent. Tracking dogs are screened and trained. They are aggressive trackers and eager to please their handler.

Knowledge of the following sensory traits and how the dog uses them helps the evader to think ahead of the dog:

Sight – A dog's vision is the lesser of its sensing abilities. It sees in black and white and has difficulty spotting static objects at more than 50m (164ft). Dogs can spot moving objects at considerable distances, however. They do not look up unless they are straining up a tree. A dog's night vision is no better than man's.

Hearing – A dangerous problem for the evader is the dog's ability to hear. Dogs can hear 40 times better than humans, and can hear quieter and higher frequencies than humans. Even more dangerous is their ability to locate the source of the sound.

Smell – The dog's sense of smell is about 900 times better than a human's. It is by far the greatest asset to hunter teams and the largest threat to the evader. Tracker dogs follow the microscopic body scent particles that continually fall from the human body and settle on the ground or other surfaces. Their remarkably sensitive noses will follow the survivor/evader's previous route as accurately as if he had drawn a map for the dog. There are ways to slow down, confuse and even defeat tracker dogs. However, using distracting or irritating odours (for example, CS powder or pepper) bothers the dog for only three to five minutes. After the dog has recovered from this distraction, he can pick up a cold trail even quicker.

The dog's powerful sense of smell allows it to form 'scent pictures'. The scent pictures are made up of several sources of smell.

• Individual scent. This is the most important scent when it comes to tracking. Vapours from body secretions work their way through the evader's shoes onto the ground. Sweat from other parts of the body rubs off onto vegetation and other objects. Scent is even left in the air.

• Reinforcing scent. Objects are introduced to the dog that reinforce the scent as it relates to the evader. Some reinforcing scents could be on the evader's clothing or boots, or the same material as is used in his clothing. Even boot polish can help the dog.

Above: Tracker dogs not only have a well developed sense of smell but also acute hearing. They can detect the scent of an escaper and evader from a variety of sources, including broken vegetation and turned soil.

- Ecological scent. For the dog, the most important scent comes from the earth itself. By far, the strongest smells come from disturbances in ecology such as crushed insects, bruised vegetation and broken ground. Over varied terrain, dogs can smell particles and vapours that are constantly carried by the evader wherever he walks.

Fortunately for the evader, the conditions will never be ideal for the tracker dog teams. During training, they become familiar with the difficulties they will face and learn to deal with them. The following conditions are favourable for tracker and dog teams.

a) Fresh scent. This is probably the most important factor for tracker teams. The fresher the scent, the greater chances of success.

b) Verified starting point. If trackers have a definite scent to introduce to the dogs, it helps the dogs to follow the correct trail.

c) Unclean evader. The sweat from an unclean evader leaves a more distinctive scent.

d) Fast-moving evader. A fast-moving evader causes more ground disturbances and individual scent from sweat.

e) Night and early morning. The air is thicker and the scent lasts longer.

f) Cool, cloudy weather. This limits evaporation of scent.

g) No wind. This keeps the scent close to the ground. It also keeps it from spreading around, allowing the dog to follow the correct route.

h) Thick vegetation. This restricts the dissemination of scent and holds the smell.

The best conditions for an evader to throw off a dog tracker team are:

a) Heat. This causes rapid evaporation of scent.

b) Unverified start point. The dogs may follow the wrong route or scent.

c) Low humidity. Scent does not last as long.

d) Dry ground. Dry ground does not retain scent.

e) Wind. Wind disperses scent and causes the dog to track downwind.

f) Heavy rain. This washes the scent away.

g) Distracting scents. These take the dog's attention away from the trail. Some of these scents are blood, meat, manure, farmland and populated areas.

h) Covered scent. Some elements in nature cause the scent picture to be partially or completely covered. Examples are sand that can blow over the tracks and help to disguise the track; snow and ice that can form over the track and make it nearly impossible to follow; and water. Water is one of the most difficult conditions for a tracker dog team. However, water that is shallow, especially if rocks or vegetation protrude, can produce a trail that a dog can follow with varied degrees of success.

AVOIDING THE DOGS

Among the techniques the soldier can use to evade dog tracker teams are:

a) Use a vehicle or even a bicycle. This will not only break the scent chain, but will put the evader further ahead of the pack much quicker and with less fatigue.

b) On foot, follow an erratic path through tangled undergrowth. This usually tangles the running lead of the dog and its handler, slowing them down.

c) The survivor/evader should use well-travelled animal or human tracks. Even better, he should follow an erratic path through a farmyard, as a large collection of new scent may temporarily confuse the dog and hinder progress.

d) On reaching water, he should not just cross it. Walk in running water for a short distance before exiting on a part of the bank where the trail will not show.

e) If there are only narrow waterways such as ditches, with still water in them, he should walk in them but cross diagonally, doubling back at least once to confuse the dog.

f) If practical, he should wash regularly, but never use anything scented.

Below: Italian *Carabinieri* use a tracker dog to search a mountainous area. In terrain like this, or in woodland and scrub, a dog is invaluable, allowing comparatively small search teams to work the area.

g) If the evader cannot wash, he should roll around over the ground he is traversing to add country scents to his own. However, remember that a man who has rolled in a dung heap smells just like a man who has rolled in a dung heap to a well-trained tracker dog with a good nose.

h) He should not allow himself to come into contact with strongly smelling substances such as smoke or animal droppings. If an article of clothing becomes contaminated and has to be discarded, he makes sure it is buried or, better still, hidden under rocks in a stream. He should also wash hair and skin if it is contaminated.

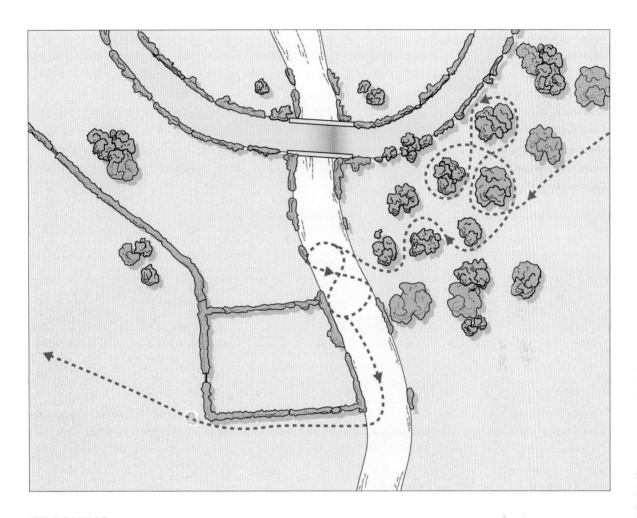

TRACKING

Movement in enemy-held territory is a very slow and deliberate process. The slower the soldier moves and the more careful he is, the better. His best security will be using his senses. He uses his eyes and ears to detect people before they detect him, and makes frequent listening halts. In daylight, the trained soldier observes a section of his route before he moves along it. The distance he travels before he hides will depend on the enemy situation, his health, the terrain, the availability of cover and concealment for hiding, and the amount of darkness left.

He must camouflage signs that he has passed, especially footprints. This is because the most common form of track to find and easiest to follow are the markings left on the ground. It is known by some trackers as ground spoor. An even better find for an experienced tracker is a full bootprint (a confirmed spoor). With a consecutive pair of prints, the tracker can tell how fast the evader is travelling, what distance he is covering and even if he is carrying a load. Despite the boot probably having the same tread pattern as the other soldiers in the unit,

Above: To evade tracker dogs, move in a convoluted pattern around vegetation, in and out of streams, and across walls and fences. This is the classic method of creating a confusing scent trail.

31

Above: Indications to a tracker where his quarry has passed include marks on vegetation, broken branches, discarded food containers, displaced stones, branches and leaves, and footprints that have been over trodden by wildlife.

individual wear marks and tread damage make boots as individual as fingerprints. Consequently, the soldier avoids walking on soft muddy ground. Instead, he tries to find hard, rocky surfaces. He must remember, though, not to disturb loose rocks as these would give a tracker recognizable, though less useful, ground spoor.

Of course there will be times when the soldier/evader will have no choice but to walk on soft or muddy ground, so he applies the following techniques. They may only temporarily confuse trackers, but they will gain valuable time. The soldier should:

a) Walk legs astride on the harder ridges on either side of well-used, soft, muddy paths.

b) Step carefully into existing footprints.

c) Walk backwards or on tiptoe.

d) Walk in a stream, remembering not to leave scuff marks or other ground spoor on the bank as he enters or leaves the stream.

Spoor above the ground or overhead may not be as easy to spot as ground spoor, but a good tracker will find it nevertheless. The rules are:

a) Don't break branches blocking a track – gently bend them aside.

b) If they can not be bent, go under, over or around them.

c) Take care not to snag or tear clothing, do not hurry. Check that small pieces of cloth or telltale fibres have not been left behind.

COUNTER-TRACKING PROCEDURES

There are other simple counter-tracking techniques that the survivor/evader can employ. While moving from close terrain to open terrain, the soldier walks past a big tree (30cm/12in) in diameter or larger) toward the open area for three to five paces. Then he walks backward to the forward side of the tree and makes a 90° change of direction, passing the tree on its forward side. He must step carefully and leave as little sign as possible.

If this is not the direction in which he wants to go, he changes direction again about 50m (164ft) away, using the same technique. The purpose of this is to draw the enemy tracker into the open area, thus causing him to search in the wrong place.

When approaching a trail, and at about 100m (328ft) from it, the soldier should change his direction of movement and approach it at an angle of 45°. On arriving at the trail, he moves along it for about 20–30m (66–98ft), leaving several signs of his presence. Then he walks backward along the trail to the point where he joined it. At that point, he crosses the trail and leaves no sign of his leaving it.

Next he moves about 100m (328ft) at an angle of 45°, but this time on the other side of the trail and in the reverse of his approach. When changing direction back to his original line of march, the big tree technique can be used. The purpose of this technique is to draw the enemy tracker along the easier trail. He has, by changing direction before reaching the trail, indicated that the trail is his new line of march.

When his direction of movement parallels a stream, the evader uses the stream to deceive an enemy tracker. Some tactics that will help elude a tracker are as follows:

Below: Wading along streams is one technique for throwing off a human or tracker dog. However, care should be taken since rocks below the surface can be slippery and the current fast.

HIDING IN WATER

A well-trained soldier should never attempt to hide in water. In films and popular fiction, the hero dips underwater to hide, breathing through a reed. The tracker dog team will find where the evader has entered the water and then the handler will fan left or right and find a place for the dog to pick up your trail on one side of the bank or the other. If they find no trail, they know that the survivor/evader is under water.

Water takes away body heat at a phenomenal rate, about seven times faster than air. Natural body temperature is about 37°C (98.6°F), so even if the water is a comfortable 23°C (74°F),

the evader will suffer from hypothermia in time. The dog team and search team will wait, and the evader will freeze. Moreover, the evader will have to get deep enough that they can't see him through the water. Breathing will also become laboured. He will exhale carbon dioxide, not all of which will clear the bamboo or reed. Breathing back his carbon dioxide will eventually lead to oxygen depletion and suffocation.

Below: The current in this fast-flowing stream is an extra hazard for a soldier as he crawls under a road bridge. Even after he has emerged, water-soaked clothes can chill him in cold weather.

- Stay in the stream for 100–200m (328–656ft).
- Stay in the centre of the stream and in deep water.
- Look out for rocks or roots near the banks that are not covered with moss or vegetation, and exit from the stream at that point.
- Walk out backwards on soft ground.
- Walk up a small, vegetation-covered tributary and exit from it.

The soldier must take care when running along streams, since he runs a tremendous risk of injury because all the rocks on the bottom are slippery. He will also move more slowly in water than on land.

CAMOUFLAGE

Until he reaches rescue or safety, a soldier or airman evading the enemy will have to stay as inconspicuous as possible. This is where the art of camouflage comes in.

The two major factors in personal camouflage are camouflage discipline and camouflage construction. Discipline is doing what is necessary to construct camouflage and maintain that camouflage. The evader/survivor should observe the area as he moves through it and change his camouflage to conform to the local vegetation or terrain. He should always check his partner, who will in turn check him, so that they maintain their level of camouflage. Any natural camouflages should be changed if they wilt or change colour over time.

Camouflage construction is the practical techniques of camouflage, and does not exclusively mean hiding from view. For example, a form of 'camouflage' is to trick the enemy into false conclusions about the location or identity of the soldier. In some theatres of operations, or during long overland movements, camouflage may include the use of disguises, such as simply adopting native dress and moving during hours of limited visibility so as to fool observers. A more elaborate plan, requiring more practice and familiarity with the area, would include walking, sitting, dressing and behaving as the local populace. The soldier must understand that disguising is a very difficult technique and is usually not worth the effort.

Visually blending into the environment is the ideal form of camouflage, and is achieved by skilfully matching personal camouflage with the surrounding area to a point where the soldier is part of the background. Blending is generally best achieved with bland colours, not dramatic patterns. Likely weather conditions for the duration of the mission must be taken into account, since this could affect the quantity and type of camouflage used. It will also affect the sequence and timing of camouflage maintenance – heat will dry out natural camouflage faster than damp weather.

The rain will cause fabrics to become darker as they become wetter. Changes from damp to snow will cause a complete change in camouflage requirements. Terrain patterns will also vary during the mission. The terrain, or mission

Below: It is essential to work in pairs when applying camouflage paint to faces – even with the aid of a mirror, a soldier will miss areas like the back of his neck, below his chin or his ears.

backdrop, at the objective may be different to that along the route to and from the objective. Again the soldier must go to the unit intelligence officer or NCO and receive as much information on the mission area as possible.

There are two basic materials that can be used for camouflage: natural (preferred) and artificial. The soldier must also consider where the material is to be applied. Is it to be applied to the skin or to the uniform? What are the dangers of parasites in the area and what is the make up of the ground materials? These will affect decisions on the materials that he will use for camouflage and where he will apply them. Natural camouflage for the skin could cause problems for the soldier later in the mission. Due to this, the soldier must be aware of the problems in the use of certain natural skin camouflage materials.

NATURAL CAMOUFLAGE

A readily available natural camouflage is grass. Grass can be used to produce a natural dye by simmering it in water for about an hour (one cup of grass to two cups of water), and the resulting dye can be applied to the skin. This would be an emergency-use item only, as the grass dye is semi-permanent in nature. This means that the dyed skin would have to be sloughed off for the dye to disappear, resulting in temporary blotching. The survivor/evader should also be aware of any caustic sap that may be in some grasses.

Grass attached to the clothing is a must when moving through grassland areas. The problem with grass is that it should not be applied in long pieces because short is better. Long grass attached to a uniform projects above the rest of the grass as the soldier moves through it, and especially when he has to observe through the top portion of grass. He should never look over anything if it can be avoided. The second problem with long sections of grass is that they bend over when attached to a uniform, thus creating a texture problem – horizontal textures and patterns in a predominately vertical world. Another problem that the soldier must be aware of is that grass is made up of two colours and the soldier must present the correct colour to the target area or an observer will see a colour error in the area.

As with grass, leaves can be used as a natural camouflage for both skin and uniform, and are also used to make a dye. All of the same cautions apply as to the semi-permanence of the dyes and the caustic nature of some leaves. As with grass, there is a dark and light side to leaves, although with leaves this difference is even more pronounced. Soldiers also need to note when they move from a three-lobed

Above: Lightly camouflaged with natural materials, US National Guardsmen hug the ground during a night exercise. The man in the right foreground has luminous tape attached to the back of his combat cap to assist in night operations.

leaf area to a single-lobed leaf area. In short, they must match the leaf camouflage with the surrounding vegetation as they move. This is a basic part of camouflage discipline. Even in a flower garden, the soldier must not use points of colour as camouflage, such as flowers. Points of colour catch the light and will attract the observer as soon as the survivor/evader using them makes a move.

Other items which can produce camouflaging skin dyes are the bark from trees, some saps, animal blood, coffee and tea (at various strengths), rock paint and mud. All have problems, but can be used in an emergency when nothing else is available. Examples of potentially dangerous dyes would, of course, include blood, although parasites, bacteria and other life-threatening organisms can also live in mud. The survivor/evader must know the area before using mud. Mud from very alkaline soils can cause skin burning after a short period of time. This burn would not be felt until it was too late and the resulting reaction could cause a mission failure.

Like mud, regular dirt and sand can be used on the skin or on the uniform as camouflage when appropriate. Rubbing two rocks together and adding water makes rock paint. This only works with certain 'soft' stones and the soldier should be warned that the camouflage will come off with sweat. A self-renewing dye is male facial hair – a beard will break up the face silhouette.

ARTIFICIAL CAMOUFLAGE

While natural camouflage is preferred, artificial camouflage will be issued as standard to soldiers, either through uniform or cosmetic skin camouflages. There are a number of items now available for camouflaging the skin. The first and most obvious is the military standard camouflage sticks. In the US Army, there are three sticks. However, the soldier only needs concern himself with two, the reason being, that there are but four colours available in the US Army sticks. Those colours are Loam, White, Light Green and Sand. The three sticks consist of loam and light

CAMOUFLAGE PATTERNS

There are three types of camouflage pattern used by the soldier. Striping, the first type, is accomplished through use of regular or irregular stripes. This pattern is used when in heavily wooded areas and leafy vegetation is scarce. Blotching is the next technique, also called splotching; this is used when the area is thick with leafy vegetation. The 'blotches' should be large and irregular. If they are too small, the effect is lost at a distance. The soldier should remember that at distance most small patterns blend and the eye takes in the dominant colour. Combination is the last and is used when moving through changing terrain. It is normally the best all-around pattern. Soldiers and survivor/evaders should always apply camouflage in pairs, and continuously re-check their partners and themselves.

green, sand and light green, and loam and white. The loam and white stick with the light green and sand stick gives the soldier all of the colours available. Use of the military sticks are a simple matter of rubbing on and rubbing off the skin in one action.

The soldier can use insect repellent to soften the sticks, which has the added benefit of keeping off aggressive insects. When using camouflage sticks, the soldier should always look at the colours around him before applying and should avoid the trap of going too dark. This is a common problem and it is aggravated in the field by the tendency of the soldier to cast a shadow upon himself while in position. Camouflage sticks or face paints are used to cover all exposed areas of skin, such as face (including ears), hands and the back of the neck. The rule is: 'if it is exposed, then it should be camouflaged'. The parts of the face that form shadows should be lightened and the parts that shine should be darkened, thus forming a sort of 'negative' of the normal appearance of the face.

From camouflage, we now turn to methods of attracting rescue, the ideal objective of any evasion situation.

Above: What every downed pilot fears – local people who know the area intimately. Iraqis during the 2003 Iraq War conduct a sweep to search for USAF aircrew who are believed to have ejected over the area.

COMMUNICATION

There are two main ways to get attention or to communicate – visual and audio signals. The means will depend on the evader's situation and the materials available. Whatever the means, the evader and survivor should always have visual and audio signals ready for use for attracting attention.

In a non-combat situation, he needs to find the largest available clear and flat area on the highest possible terrain. He should use as obvious a signal as he can create. On the other hand, he will have to be more discreet in combat situations. He does not want to signal and attract the enemy. He should pick an area that is visible from the air, but ensure there are hiding places nearby. The soldier should try to have a hill or other object between the signal site and the enemy to mask his signal from the enemy. He needs to undertake a thorough reconnaissance of the area to ensure there are no enemy forces nearby.

Whatever signalling technique or device he plans to use, he should know how to use it and be ready to put it into operation at short notice. If possible, he must avoid using signals or signalling techniques that increase the danger, keeping in mind that signals to his friends may alert the enemy of his presence and location. Before signalling, he must carefully weigh his rescue chances by friends against the danger of capture by the enemy. A radio is probably the surest and quickest way to let others know where he is and to let him receive their messages. He should become familiar with the radios in his unit and learn how to operate them and to send and receive broadcasts.

A trained soldier learns about a variety of other signalling techniques, devices and articles he can can use. He should think of ways in which he can adapt or change them for different environments and practice using all techniques before he needs them. Planned, pre-arranged signalling techniques may improve his chance of rescue.

Opposite: An RAF Tornado pilot using his Trimble GPS to find his location during a post-ejection escape and evasion exercise. He will then use his PRC-112 radio to call in a Combat Search and Rescue (CSAR) unit for a pickup.

SMOKE GRENADES

Smoke grenades are an instantaneous way of generating a signal. They must be kept dry at all times and care taken not to ignite the vegetation in the area where used. The British PW Defence coloured signal smoke grenade No 83 series is one example of smoke grenades and it has numerous applications, including ground and air signalling, marking of landing and dropping zones, wind speed and direction indication, and search and rescue marking.

Each No 83 series grenade consists of an extruded aluminium casing surmounted by a standard flip-up lever ignition system that has a centre-fire percussion cap. A single emission port is located centrally at the opposite end. To operate, the grenade pin is removed with the flip-up lever held against the grenade body. The striker fires the percussion cap when the lever is released. The lever can be fitted with an optional Foreign Object Damage (FOD) device to reduce hazards to aircraft or helicopters. The grenade is fully waterproof. The complete list of No 83 series grenade types is as follows:

Grenade hand 83 smoke red: N101
Grenade hand 83 smoke white: N102
Grenade hand 83 smoke green: N103
Grenade hand 83 smoke blue: N104
Grenade hand 83 smoke yellow: N105
Grenade hand 83 smoke purple: N106
Grenade hand 83 smoke orange: N107
Grenade hand 83 coloured sand: N108

Below: The Day/Night hand-held smoke flare that allows CSAR to pinpoint the position of a pilot.

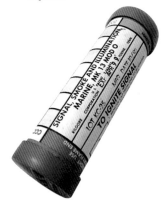

SMOKE AND FIRE

Fire is an excellent visual signal. During darkness, it is the most effective visual means for attracting attention. The soldier should attempt to build three fires in a triangle (the international distress signal) or in a straight line with about 25m (82ft) between them, constructing the unlit fires as soon as time and the situation permit and protecting them until the right moment for lighting. If he is alone, however, maintaining three fires may be difficult, so one signal fire will suffice.

When constructing signal fires, he considers his geographic location. If in a jungle, he finds a natural clearing or the edge of a stream where he can build fires that the jungle foliage will not hide. If in a snow-covered area, he can either clear the ground of snow or make a platform on which to build the fire so that melting snow will not extinguish it.

A burning tree (tree torch) is another way to attract attention. A highly visible signal is created by setting pitch-bearing trees afire, even when green. The soldier can get other types of trees to burn by placing dry wood in the lower branches and igniting it so that the flames flare up and ignite the surrounding foliage. Before the primary tree is consumed, he should cut and add green branches to the fire to produce more smoke. Isolated trees are the best tree torches, as the flames do not spread to other trees to start a forest fire.

During daylight, the evader can build a smoke generator and use smoke to gain attention. The international distress signal is three columns of smoke. He should try to create a colour of smoke that contrasts with the background; dark smoke against a light background, and vice versa. If he practically smothers a large fire with green leaves or moss, or sprinkles on a little water, the fire will produce white smoke.

If he adds rubber or oil-soaked rags to a fire, he will get black smoke. In a desert environment, smoke hangs close to the ground, but a pilot can spot it in the open terrain. Smoke signals are effective only on comparatively calm, clear days. High winds, rain or snow disperse smoke, lessening its chances of being seen.

FLARES AND PYROTECHNICS

Pen flares are part of the kit in an aircrew survival vest, but some versions can be bought commercially for use by climbers and yachtsmen. The device consists of a pen-shaped gun with a flare attached by a nylon cord. When fired, the pen flare sounds like a pistol shot and fires the flare up to about 150m (492ft). It is about 3cm (1.2in) in diameter.

There are two types of pen flare widely in service with US and other forces. One is a threaded projector with the projectiles being contained in a cloth bandoleer. Each of the signals listed below may be fired from a hand-held projector while encompassed in the bandoleer.

- Red illumination ground signal, M187.

- White illumination ground signal, M188.
- Green illumination ground signal, M189.
- Amber illumination ground signal, M190.

The contents and operation of the first type of pen flare break down as follows:

1) Contents. The projector and the bandoleer plus seven projectiles/signals make up the signal kit. All signals may be obtained and fired separately. The M185 red signal kit contains only red signals. The M186 signal kit contains three red, two white and two green signals.

2) Operation. Select the signal to be fired by colour. If the bandoleer contains more than one signal of the chosen colour, use the one farthest from the

Below: With a hand-held radio and smoke flare, a member of a search and rescue team signals to a helicopter from the top of Helm Crag, Cumbria, UK during a search and rescue exercise.

LIGHTSTICKS

Types of Lightstick available include:

10cm (4in), general purpose (green)

15cm (6in), 30 minutes high intensity (yellow)

15cm (6in), 12 hours general purpose (green)

15cm (6in), 12 hours (red)

15cm (6in), 8 hours (blue)

15cm (6in), 12 hours (yellow)

15cm (6in), 12 hours (orange)

15cm (6in), non-visible (infra-red)

Personnel marker light 8 hours (green-yellow)

Combat light device (holder for 15cm/6in lights)

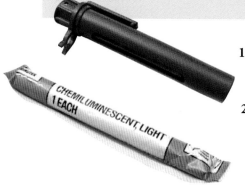

Above: The Cyalume Lightstick (lower) and the Combat Light Device (top) provide waterproof light without heat, and can be concealed or attached to posts or equipment.

lanyard. Remove and discard the plastic cap. Cock the projector by moving the trigger to the safety slot. Carefully thread the projector onto the signal, taking care not to dislodge the trigger from the safety slot. Aim in the chosen direction. Fire by moving the trigger to the bottom of the firing slot and releasing it with a snap. If the expended signal is on the end of the bandoleer, or if the signals between the expended signal and the end have been used, cut the bandoleer and discard the waste. Return the partially used kit to the barrier bag and seal with tape.

The other pen gun flare is identified by a force-fitted projector and a plastic bandoleer. With this kit, the projectiles must be removed from the bandoleer before being fired.

1) Contents. This kit contains only red illumination ground signals. The projector and the bandoleer plus seven signals make up this kit. The burning time for these signals is 10 seconds at 100,000 candlepower.

2) Operation. To operate this signal, select and remove the signal to be fired from the bandoleer using the one farthest from the lanyard. Carefully insert the nozzle end of the signal into the projector as far as it will go. Fire by pulling the trigger knob to the rear of the slot and releasing with a snap. Retain the bandoleer for future use. Return the partially used kit to the plastic bag and seal with tape.

The British Wallop Defence Systems 16mm Mini-Signal is very similar to the above pen flares. It consists of a block containing eight encapsulated signals plus a 'safe-fire' mechanism. In use, the safe-fire mechanism is rotated, connected onto a locating rail below the flare block and indexed to below a selected flare. The block and firing mechanism are then held vertically and the safe-fire mechanism is then squeezed to release a flare. The Mini-Signal can only be fired vertically to prevent possible use as an offensive weapon. White, red and green (or mixed) signal colours are available. Each signal burns for up to 4 seconds after reaching a deployment height of 100m (328ft). The signals are visible in bright daylight to a range of up to 1500m (4921ft).

The British PW Defence Day and Night distress signal is a dual-purpose compact distress signal designed to military specifications. It can produce an orange smoke to attract attention in daylight, and a red flare to summon help during darkness. The signal is visible from at least 5000m (16,404ft) by day and 8000m (26,246ft) by night in good conditions. It consists of a yellow protective outer case with an improved tactile marking of two raised ribs around the flare end for easy recognition in darkness. The red protective end caps, which are now interchangeable, are sealed by waterproof 'O' rings. Either end can be fired independently by means of a pull-ring percussion striker mechanism and the unused end stored until it is required. The Day and Night's versatility and compact shape enables it to be carried easily as a personal distress signal. It is suitable for infantry, for use in aircraft emergency and personal survival packs, especially in maritime situations, and as a diver's personal distress signal.

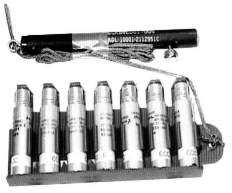

Left: The aircrew pen flare kit. It is compact enough to fit into the survival vest and quick and simple to operate. Similar types of equipment are available for sailors and climbers.

STROBE LIGHTS

At night, a survivor can use a torch or flashlight or a strobe light to send an SOS to an aircraft. When using a strobe light, he must take care to prevent the pilot from mistaking it for incoming ground fire. The strobe light flashes 60 times per minute. The superb ACR Electronics MS-2000(M) is a state-of-the-art strobe light with features including:

- Shield that extends/retracts for omni- or uni-directional visibility
- Waterproof down to 15.3m (50ft); a 60m (200ft) diver version is available
- IR filter blocks all visible light (lets through only IR light)
- Raised polarity indicators allow correct battery replacement in low or no visibility conditions
- New braided steel retainer keeps battery door from being lost
- Operates on two standard alkaline AA batteries
- Blue filter distinguishes strobe from ground fire when in place

SPECIFICATIONS

Size: (11.4 x 5.6 x 3.3cm) 4.5 x 2.2 x 1.1in

Weight: 115g (4.0oz) without batteries

Light Output: 250,000 peak lumens per flash

Flash Rate: 50 ± 10 per minute

Light Dispersion: White – omni-directional;
    IR – omni-directional;
    Blue – uni-directional

Operating Life: eight hours minimum – strobe;
    two hours minimum – incandescent

Visibility: Military tested at a distance of 9.6km
    (6 miles) on a clear dark night

Waterproof: To a depth of 15.3m (50ft);
    61m (200ft) diver version available

Batteries: 2 AA alkaline or lithium batteries

Case Colour: Black with olive drab flashguard

Construction: Case, lens and flashguard –
    high-impact polycarbonate;
    IR filter – butyrate

Activation: Spark-proof magnetic reed switch

Whatever the system, the soldier should have the pen flare ready for immediate use with the flare attached – leaving the gun uncocked – and worn on a cord or chain around the neck. He needs to be prepared to fire it in front of a search aircraft and be ready with a secondary signal, and to take cover in case the pilot mistakes the flare for enemy fire.

LIGHTSTICKS

American-developed Cyalume Lightsticks are strictly not pyrotechnics, since they do not burn, but these devices must be considered under this heading since they perform the same function as pyrotechnic flares. The Cyalume Lightstick is a sealed plastic tube containing a liquid chemical composition which is inert until the tube is bent between the fingers and shaken. It then emits light without heat, flames or sparks; depending upon the type of light in use, this emission will last from 30 minutes to 12 hours. The lights are provided in various colours so that they may be used for warning, signalling or illumination purposes. In military use, they can be applied as minefield, route or perimeter markers, drop-zone markers, river-crossing guides, for map reading, or for illuminating the interior of command posts or communication centres. The lights work equally well under water and can be used by demolition frogmen. A rugged plastic carrying case (the Combat Light Device) has a clip where it can be attached to clothes or equipment and is fitted with an adjustable shutter, which means the light can be regulated or occluded as desired.

There is also a Personnel Marker Light that can be attached to flotation devices; this clips to the clothing or a lifejacket and carries a permanently fitted Cyalume Lightstick. This can be activated by squeezing it, after which it acts as a marker visible up to 1600m (5249ft) and lasts for eight hours.

STAR CLUSTERS

Red is the international distress colour, so if star cluster flare ammunition is available, the red star cluster should be used whenever possible. Any colour, however, will let rescuers know where an evader or survivor is located. Star clusters reach a height of 200–215m (656–705ft), burn for an average of 6–10 seconds, and descend at a rate of 14mps (46ftps).

The latest version of the Star Cluster, which can be fired from an M79 or M203 low-velocity launcher, is the M585. It is intended for illumination and signalling with less weight and greater accuracy than hand-held signals. The cartridge is a fixed round of ammunition consisting of a projectile assembly and a cartridge case assembly. The projectile has a one-piece, hollow aluminium body with a rotating band. A plastic ogive (nose cone), embossed with a raised W for night identifications of payload colour and five raised dots to identify a cluster round, is

Below: Care should be taken when using a signal mirror not to blind the pilot of an approaching helicopter. Signal mirrors are an invaluable CSAR tool since they have an infinite life, unlike radios or pyrotechnics.

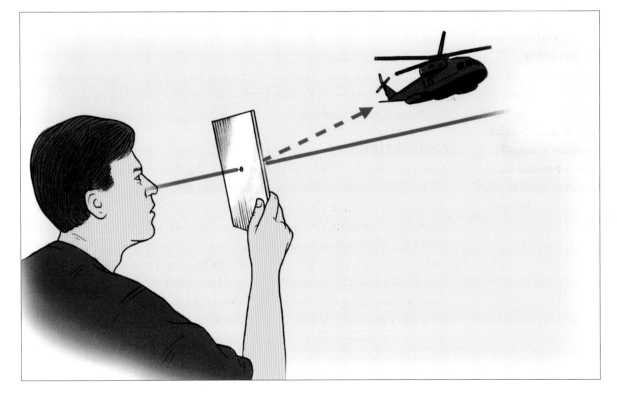

Above: Senior Airman Tim Tweeter, a pararescue specialist from the US 38th Air Rescue Squadron, sits in tall weeds and fires a smoke flare to signal a rescue helicopter.

snapped into an O-ring in the front opening of the projectile cavity. The cavity contains an illuminant candle assembly of five white star charges and a black-powder ejection charge. The star charges are contained in phenolic-coated Kraft paper and mounted on a base plug of similar material over the ejection charge. A five-second delay pyrotechnic ignition charge is fitted into the centre of the projectile base.

Star Parachute Flares reach a height of 200–215m (656–705ft) and descend at a rate of 2.1mps (7ftps). The M126 (red) burns for about 50 seconds and the M127 (white) about 25 seconds. At night, these flares can be seen at ranges of 48–56km (30–35 miles).

REFLECTIVE SIGNALS

On a sunny day, a mirror is the soldier's best signalling device. Pilots have reported seeing signal mirror flashes at distances of 160km (100 miles). If the survivor/evader does not have a mirror, he should polish his canteen cup, his belt buckle or a similar object that will reflect the sun's rays, and direct sunlight flashes from an area secure from enemy observation. If he has a Mk 3 signal mirror, he follows the instructions on its back. The evader should not flash a signal mirror rapidly because a pilot may mistake the flashes for enemy fire. He should not direct

the beam into a rescue aircraft's cockpit for more than a few seconds, as it may blind the pilot. Haze, ground fog and mirages may make it hard for a pilot to spot signals from a flashing object. So, if possible, the soldier gets to the highest point in his area when signalling. If he can't determine the aircraft's location, he flashes his signal in the direction of the aircraft noise.

The evader must wear the signal mirror on a cord or chain around his neck so that it is ready for immediate use. However, he should be sure the glass side is against his body so that it will not flash; the enemy might see the inadvertent signal.

OTHER VISUAL SIGNALS
VS-17 Panel
During daylight, the soldier can also use a VS-17 coloured panel to signal. He should place the orange side up, as it is easier to see from the air than the violet side. Flashing the panel will make it easier for the aircrew to spot. He can use any bright orange or violet cloth as a substitute for the VS-17.

Clothing
Spreading clothing on the ground or in the top of a tree is another way to signal. The survivor should select articles whose colour will contrast with the natural surroundings, and arrange them in a geometric pattern to make them more likely to attract attention.

Natural Material
If he lacks other means, he can use natural materials to form a symbol or message that can be seen from the air. He can build mounds that cast shadows, using brush, foliage of any type, rocks or snow blocks. In snow-covered areas, snow can be tramped down to form letters or symbols and the depressions filled with contrasting material (twigs or branches). In sand, boulders, vegetation or seaweed are used to create a symbol or message. In brush-covered areas, the soldier cuts out patterns in the vegetation or sears the ground. In tundra, digging trenches or turning the sod upside down serves the same purpose. In any terrain, the key is to use contrasting materials that will make the symbols visible to aircrews.

Sea Dye Markers
All US military aircraft involved in operations near or over water will normally carry a water survival kit that contains sea dye markers. If a downed pilot is in a water survival situation, he can use the sea dye markers during daylight to indicate his location. These spots of dye stay conspicuous for about three hours, except in very rough seas. He should use them only if he is in a friendly area, and deploy them only when he hears or sights an aircraft. Sea dye markers are also very effective on snow, where they can be used to write distress code letters.

Right: USAF aircrew during a CSAR exercise use the very effective combination of high- and low-tech equipment – a PRC-112 radio and signal mirror. The mirror allows the approaching pilot to get an exact fix on the pilot and navigator.

AUDIO AND RADIO COMMUNICATIONS

Radios, whistles and gunshots are some of the methods a soldier can use to signal his presence to rescuers. The evader may use rifle or pistol shots combined with tracer ammunition to signal search aircraft. However, care should be taken not to fire the ammunition in front of the aircraft. As with pen flares, the evader should be ready to take cover if the pilot mistakes his tracers for enemy fire. Three shots fired at distinct intervals usually indicate a distress signal. He should not use this technique in enemy territory since the enemy will surely come to investigate shots.

Whistles provide an excellent method of close-range signalling. In some documented cases, they have been heard up to 1.6km (1 mile) away. Manufactured whistles have more range than a human whistle. However, for longer-range communication the best tool is the radio.

The US AN/PRC-90 survival radio is a part of the US Army aviator's survival vest. The AN/PRC-112 will eventually replace the AN/PRC-90. Both radios can transmit either tone or voice. ACR Electronics is a leading supplier of the PRC-90-2 and PRC-106 survival transceivers that are standard equipment with military, law enforcement and search-and-rescue organizations around the world. The improved PRC-90-2 survival transceiver is familiar to most military aviators as the rugged, hand-held survival radio that has saved the lives of thousands of downed pilots and crew members. It has voice and beacon capability on the military distress frequency of 243.0 with voice-only on 282.8 MHz.

The PRC-106 – a derivative of the PRC-90-2 – provides both beacon and voice capability on the civil and military distress frequencies of 121.5 and 243.0 MHz.

The latest US equipment is the Combat Survivor Evader Locator (CSEL) system, a secure world-wide communication and location system to search for and rescue downed pilots in combat environments. The CSEL is a lightweight, low-power, over-the-horizon radio with an integrated GPS receiver.

MAYDAY PROCEDURE

If the survivor/evader can contact a friendly aircraft with a radio, he should guide the pilot to his location. The fact that the soldier has made contact with rescuers does not mean he is safe. He should follow instructions and continue to use sound survival and evasion techniques until he is rescued. The following format should be followed when contacting rescue aircraft:

1) 'Mayday, Mayday.'
2) Gives call sign (if any).
3) Gives name.
4) Gives location.
5) Gives number of survivors.
6) Provides details about available landing sites.
7) Provides further details such as medical aid or other specific types of help needed.

Opposite: Ground-to-air signals are useful for communicating with aircraft.

A – Serious injury

B – Need medical supplies

C – Unable to proceed

D – Need food and water

E – Need firearms

F – Need map/compass

G – Need signal lamp

H – Indicate direction to proceed

I – Am proceeding in this direction

J – Will attempt takeoff

K – Aircraft seriously damaged

L – Safe to land here

M – Need food

N – All well

O – No

P – Yes

Q – Not understood

R – Need engineer

Such sophisticated devices may be available, but in an emergency any type of military radio can be used. The working range of the different radios varies depending on the altitude of the receiving aircraft, terrain, vegetation density, weather, battery strength, type of radio and interference. To obtain maximum performance from radios, the evader should use the following procedures:

- Try to transmit only in clear, unobstructed terrain. Since radios are line-of-sight communications devices, any terrain between the radio and the receiver will block the signal. However, terrain (and particularly metal power lines) can be used to screen signals from enemy radio direction finding (RDF) equipment.
- Keep the antenna at right angles to the rescuing aircraft or search party. There is no signal from the tip of the antenna.
- Try not to let the antenna touch clothing, the body, foliage or the ground. Such contact greatly reduces the range of the signal.

It is vital that the survivor/evader conserves battery power, turning the radio off when it is not in use. In cold weather, he should keep the battery inside his clothing when not using the radio – cold quickly drains the battery's power. Nor should he expose the battery to extreme heat such as desert sun. High heat may cause the battery to explode. The radio and battery must be kept as dry as possible, as water may destroy the circuitry. The soldier should refrain from transmitting or receiving constantly. In hostile territory, transmissions must be kept short to avoid enemy RDF.

LOCATOR BEACONS

An advanced electronic system of attracting rescue is the locator beacon. The SARBE 406 Personal Locator Beacon (PLB) from Signature Industries Ltd of the UK is a good example of the ruggedized system that uses the well-established SARBE automatic activation mechanism. It is compatible with ejector seats and life-raft inflation mechanisms.

The SARBE 406 transmits to the KOSPAS-SARSAT (Search-and-Rescue Satellite Aided Tracking System) global satellite system. It has an over-the-horizon performance and alerts rescue forces as to the identity of the beacon and the area of the incident. A swept tone on 121.5 Mhz is also transmitted, allowing direction-finding by surface and airborne rescue units, and a strobe light is incorporated to assist final location in darkness. Visual indication of operation is provided by LEDs at the top of the beacon. The SARBE 406 digital identity code (for transmission to satellite) can be reprogrammed by the user with a laptop computer via IR input and output ports.

The Australian Warrendi Personal Locator Beacon (PLB) was designed to meet a specification developed by the Royal Australian Air Force's Life Support Engineering Agency. The PLB weighs 1100g (2.4lb) and measures 173 x 103 x 49mm (7 x 4 x 2in). Central to the capability of the PLB is its ability to alert on

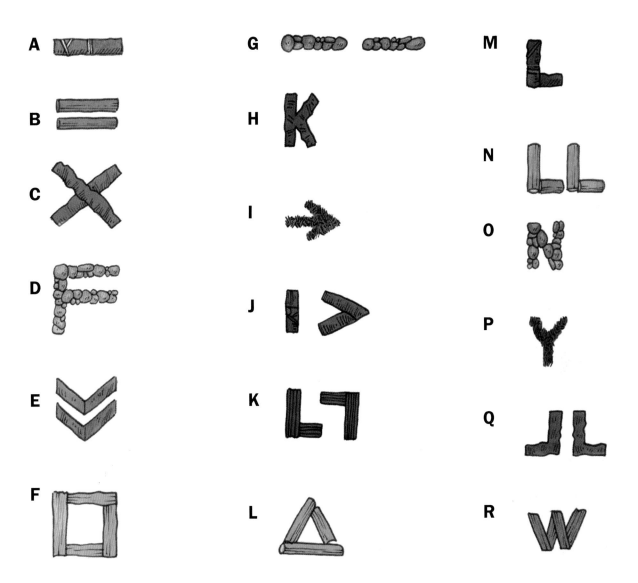

several frequencies simultaneously. In addition to the KOSPAS/SARSAT satellite, the PLB also offers alternative operating modes using military distress frequencies and methods of operation optimized for direction-finding search.

Use of a fully sealed electronics enclosure protects the circuitry from deterioration during extended storage and built-in test facilities can be used periodically to verify full operational readiness. Other features include: a radio communication function; synthetic voice transmission of GPS-derived survivor's position; and compatibility with existing ship and aircraft VHF/UHF AM radio receivers.

Above: A USAF Major uses a PRC-90 during a search and rescue training exercise in Thailand. He holds a Lensatic compass in his right hand and is wearing a survival vest.

LAND-BASED GLOBAL POSITIONING SYSTEMS

The chances of an on-the-run soldier, sailor or airman being located and rescued have been revolutionized in recent years by the Global Positioning System (GPS). For centuries, navigators on sea and land, and later in the air, used the sun, stars or compass to plot and follow planned routes. On land it was also possible with a map or aerial photographs to identify the terrain and features to give an accurate navigation 'fix' or a precise location. On the open sea, rolling desert or in thick jungle, this was almost impossible without using a compass and map.

In January 1980, navigation changed forever when the US Department of Defense (DoD) launched the first of what would eventually be 24 NAVSTAR satellites which form the building blocks of GPS. The lead on the programme came from the US Air Force, but the utility of GPS is now acknowledged by naval and army users. (This despite the fact that in the early days of GPS navigation, a rumour persisted among US Navy aviators that if a pilot crossed the equator in an aircraft equipped with GPS navigation, the system would immediately instruct the aircraft to roll and fly upside down.) With solar panels extended, the NAVSTAR satellites are 5.2m (17ft) wide and weigh 860kg (1892lb). They circle the world at a height of 20,000km (12,427 miles), making one circumnavigation every 12 hours. They provide all-weather, common grid, worldwide navigation and timing information to land-, sea- and air--based users. Their location information is accurate to 5m (16ft). GPS can be used worldwide and is compatible with the 103 different map datums.

Users enter the way-stations, grid or longitude and latitude checkpoints on their proposed course into a GPS receiver. At the press of a button, an arrow displayed on the screen of a GPS shows whether the user should move to the left or right to remain on course, and also gives the course correction in degrees. In addition, it shows the bearing to the waypoint and how far away it is. This level of accuracy is ensured by fixes on four or more of the NAVSTAR satellites.

Commercial users of GPS, like sailors or wilderness backpackers, use what is known as the C-Code or Coarse Acquisition code, while the military use Precise Positioning (PP), or P-Code. The P-Code gives accuracies better than 10m (32ft), but is incredibly complex and constantly changing. The philosophy behind the P-Code was that very precise navigation aids could be used as a low-budget guidance for bombs or missiles by terrorists or hostile nations. Only a specifically programmed receiver is able to unscramble P-Code signals. A side effect of this security is that military users need to know approximately where they are before they lock their PPS GPS receiver onto the finely tuned transmissions. The sale of equipment which uses the Precise Positioning Service (PPS) must be cleared by the US DoD through the Foreign Military Sales (FMS) process. P-Code accuracy down to 10cm (0.3in) is invaluable for accurate targeting by Forward Air Controllers or Forward Observation Officers. With a laser range-finder or designator and GPS, they can give a very accurate target indication from their position for ground-attack aircraft, artillery or mortars.

C-Code signals are locked onto quickly, but do not give as accurate a fix as P-Code. Ironically, manufacturers of C-Code GPS managed to refine them to give a fix down to 10m (32ft), which was almost 10 times more accurate than military users had assumed C-Code GPS could deliver and quite sufficient for armoured vehicles on the move across the desert.

GPS IN THE GULF WAR

GPS was a crucial aid for Special Forces during the First Gulf War in 1991, when navigation, particularly at night, was very difficult in the desert. However, GPS did not always work effectively during Operation Desert Sabre, the allied land campaign in Iraq and Kuwait. General Patrick Cordingley, who commanded the British 7th Armoured Brigade, explained that 'First thing in the morning, and then just after dark, the satellites that provided the signals would go out of range. As a result, every morning and evening for about fifteen minutes we would get lost'.

On one evening, an Orders Group called at 19.00 hours had to be cancelled as the GPS in the vehicles carrying the officers had 'gone down'. The vehicles were in radio but not visual contact. Faced by the prospect of key officers roaming about the desert and possibly becoming lost in the darkness, the commanding officer cancelled the O Group and instructed the officers to turn round and follow their vehicle tracks back to their unit locations.

However, General Cordingley was an enthusiast for the accuracy of GPS and, explaining its merits, he said, 'They [the GPS receivers] worked so well I put in a request for hundreds more, my aim being that every infantry platoon and tank

Above: A UK PRC-085193 SARBE that allows aircrew to transmit location signals to approaching rescue aircraft and to speak to them over short ranges when they have homed in on the position.

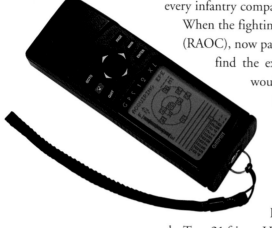

should have one. By the time the ground war started, there were at least two in every infantry company and nearly all the tanks had them'.

When the fighting was over, a major in the then Royal Army Ordnance Corps (RAOC), now part of the Royal Logistic Corps, described how he used GPS to find the exact position of buried ISO containers full of stores. 'You would turn up in the middle of the desert, get the fix on your GPS, tell the driver of the JCB (backhoe tractor) to start digging and within a minute or two there would be the container. Without GPS, they would probably have stayed there for ever'.

Though the Gulf War made the general public aware of GPS, it had in fact been used as far back as 1982 during the Falklands campaign. Captain Chris Craig, who commanded the Type 21 frigate HMS Alacrity, was equipped with GPS at a time when they were an expensive navigation novelty. Following the Gulf War, the US Army, which prior to 1991 had thought GPS would be useful only for helicopter navigation, stated that it had a requirement for 350 one-channel manpacked/vehicle sets, 63 five-channel sea sets and 4949 two-channel aircraft sets. In addition, their request for an additional 50,764 commercial grade C-Code sets and 880 aircraft sets was approved by the Department of the Army in April 1991.

The success of C-Code GPS in the Gulf War made the DoD realize how accurate commercial systems had become, and to prevent their misuse the DoD introduced the C/A-Code that uses Selective Availability, or S/A. This makes the satellite atomic clock send slightly incorrect statements about the time that the signal segment was transmitted. Though these are only a fraction of a second, they are enough to ensure that they cannot be used as a guidance system for a terrorist device.

Companies like Trimble, Silva, JRC, Raytheon, Garmin and Magellan have dominated the military and commercial GPS field. Trimble equipment includes the Centurion, installed in AFVs and helicopters, and the Miniature Underwater GPS Receiver (MUGR), which is waterproof to 20m (65ft), has six channels and is the smallest hand-held receiver, weighing only 540g (1.2lb). The Garmin GPS includes the GPS 38 hand-held land system and the GPS 45XL marine system. The Swedish Silva GPS Compass uses the Rockwell NavCore Micro Tracker tm LP, the smallest and lowest current five-channel receiver on the world market. It is the only hand-held GPS with an integral electronic compass that will give a compass bearing even if the user is stationary. Silva state that while other GPS show bearing and distance, their system points the user in the right direction.

The low budget commercial C-code GPS are generally single-channel systems which have one central receiving and processing device to handle the received time signals and other data, but this regularly has to switch over to processing the information into legs, time and waypoints. The single-channel receiver cannot

Above: The Garmin GPS12 hand-held GPS. Available to the commercial market, it weighs 269g (9.5oz) and has a battery life of 15 hours. It allows walkers, sailors and climbers to plan routes or get an accurate fix on their position.

MODERN MILITARY GPS RECEIVERS

One of the successful GPS receivers used during the Gulf War was the Magellan NAV 1000 M5, while the Magnavox MX7120 and Magnavox GPS Engine Turbo Version have also been adopted by the US Army. Collins have developed the Trooper Handheld/Vehicular GPS receiver and with it the Mission Planning Station. The Trooper is based on the Rockwell NavCor V GPS that can store up to 100 waypoints and 10 routes. It displays Speed Over Ground (SOG), Time to Go (TTG), Velocity Made Good/ground speed (VMG), Estimated Time of Arrival (ETA) and Cross Track Error (XTE). The screen is night-vision goggle compatible and sunlight readable. The Mission Planning Station for the Trooper uses a 25 MHz 486DX Toshiba T4400SXC VGA laptop computer to create and maintain libraries of waypoints and routes, which can then be transferred directly to the Trooper receiver. Waypoints that have been generated by the Trooper can be transferred to the computer library.

Above: Lt. Jim Eyre, a patrol leader with Pathfinder Platoon, using a Magellan GPS NAV1000M GPS in dense cover. GPS are invaluable where there are no obvious landmarks.

TRAPing

In August 2000, prior to deployment to the war-torn West African state of Sierra Leone, the Air Group of the Royal Navy's HMS *Ocean* developed an airborne extraction technique. With the acronym TRAP – Tactical Recovery of Aircraft & Personnel – it brought together the three types of helicopter operating from *Ocean*.

Prior to a mission, a pilot would have filled out an 'Isoprep Form'. This gave personal details known as 'the big six': name, rank, number, date of birth, blood group and religion. In addition, there was a description of physical appearance and four pieces of personal information known only to that individual, such as the name and breed of the family dog. This would ensure that the rescue helicopter would not be drawn into an ambush by an impostor, since the downed pilot could be interrogated at a safe altitude. The completed forms were held by the Air Group.

The TRAP team deployed two Sea King helicopters, each carrying a section of Marines, to land and secure the area and extract the pilot or crew. Prior to this, Lynx and Gazelle helicopters fitted with high-magnification sights would sweep the area. The Lynx also mounts the BAe Systems Avionics SS600 Series 3 Thermal Imaging equipment. The TRAP team would home on the SARBE distress beacon or radio and examine the area for any hostile forces before making the rescue.

monitor several satellites, but looks at them in turn and then makes averaging assumptions about speed and direction.

Multiplex receivers have been described as 'single channel units with a more flashy name and a bit of extra computing memory and power to do all the number crunching more rapidly'. Single-channel and multiplex systems require relatively little current and are therefore favoured for hand-held GPS. Multi-Channel receivers can range from three to 24 channels. They work very well in terrain where an antenna might be screened, since they will lock onto the nearest unobstructed satellite. They process the information faster and gives a more accurate indication of speed than a single-channel GPS.

GETTING THE MESSAGE OVER

Now that the soldier knows how to to attract his rescuers' attention, he needs to know how to give them more information. It is easier to form one symbol than to spell out an entire message, therefore he should learn the codes and symbols that all rescue teams and aircraft pilots understand.

He can use lights or flags to send an SOS – three dots, three dashes, three dots. The SOS is the internationally recognized distress signal in radio Morse code. A dot is a short, sharp pulse; a dash is a longer pulse. The soldier keeps repeating the signal until contact is made. When using flags, he holds flags on the left side for dashes and on the right side for dots.

The Ground-to-Air Emergency Code is actually five definite, meaningful symbols, each symbol being a minimum of 1m (3.2ft) wide and 6m (20ft) long. If he makes them larger, the soldier should keep the same 1:6 ratio. He ensures the signal contrasts strongly with the ground it is on and places it in an open area easily spotted from the air. When an aircraft is close enough for the pilot to see him clearly, the survivor/evader can use body movements or positions to convey a message. Once the pilot of a fixed-wing aircraft has sighted the survivor/evader, he will normally indicate he has seen him by flying low, 'wobbling' the plane and flashing his lights.

Armed and equipped with an array of survival and signalling devices, the survivor/evader may use the skills he has learned to escape from his pursuers and rendezvous with rescuers. One of the classic instances of survival and evasion occurred in 1991 during the Gulf War when an SAS team was hunted by enemy forces in the Iraqi desert. The experience of 'Bravo Two Zero' has achieved a legendary status, but it is worth looking at again for an example of professional evasion strategies before we go on to look at techniques of surviving captivity in Chapter 3.

Below: Royal Thai Air Force Sgt. Sutthiphan Jankeeree (left) and USAF Master Sgt. Joe Sitterly (right) make contact with 'friendly' forces using PRC-90 HF radios, as part of a search and rescue training exercise in Thailand, 1999.

BRAVO TWO ZERO

In the Gulf War of 1990–91, Britain's Special Air Service (SAS) helped to gather intelligence on the movement of Iraqi troop and weapons convoys. They set up road watch patrols at three points on three east–west axes, or Main Supply Routes (MSRs). The teams drawn from B Squadron consisted of eight men each, and they were inserted by helicopter about 225–290km (140–180 miles) inside Iraq.

Above: The SAS road watch patrol code named B20, or Bravo Two Zero, pose at the rear ramp of a Chinook helicopter prior to their insertion in Iraq in 1991. The men who survived have their faces blacked out to ensure security.

When the NCO commanding Road Watch South landed, he did not release the helicopter before he had assessed the terrain. This was open and flat and in the words of one Trooper, the patrol would have been 'as obvious as a turd on a billiard table'. The NCO and patrol decided that without vehicles it was a futile operation and were wisely withdrawn back to Saudi Arabia, for subsequent redeployment.

Road Watch Central realized that they too were in an exposed location, but they had released their helicopter. Worse still, their radio communications were intermittent. Fortunately, they were vehicle-mounted. The corporal in command of the patrol realized that they would have to make their way back to friendly territory, but before exiting the area they called in an air strike by US Air Force A-10 ground-attack aircraft. The patrol drove for 225km (140 miles) by night through Iraq and reached safety.

The eight-man SAS team which made up Road Watch North had the radio call-sign B20 – or. in the phonetic language used by military radio operators, Bravo Two Zero. They were not to enjoy the same good fortune as the other two groups.

During briefings, the men held a 'Chinese Parliament' to talk through all aspects of the operation – standard SAS practice. The patrol, led by Sergeant Philip 'Mitch' and codenamed Turbo, worried that just as the British airborne attack on Arnhem in 1944 had been a 'bridge too far', it was about to be sent on a 'mission too far'. The men knew that there was now a shortage of specialist equipment in theatre. They were expected to be self-sufficient for 14 days, carrying ammunition, radio, batteries, sleeping bag, spare clothing and rations. Each man would have a Bergen rucksack weighing about 75kg (165lb).

Turbo was lifted by an RAF Chinook(2) of 7 Special Forces Squadron. The helicopter crew wore Passive Night Goggles (PNG) that allowed them to fly low across Iraq at night. While they landed the team, a Coalition air raid was directed against targets to the North as cover.

Almost at once, Turbo was entangled in a firefight with local forces. The SAS patrol returned fire and dropped their Bergens to escape. They now had their personal weapons and belt order – enough to survive, but not to undertake their mission. Since Jordan was neutral but friendly to Iraq, their only option was to escape northwards overland to Syria, using compass and satellite Global Positioning System (GPS) receivers.

They moved fast at night in appalling winter weather and lay up during the day in rough 'hides' scraped in the ground. At one point, they thought they had heard an aircraft and stopped to switch on their search-and-rescue tactical beacon (TACBE), to provide a homing beacon for rescue helicopters. However, in the howling wind, rain and darkness, three men were unaware that the patrol had stopped, and pushed on.

The three-man team was further reduced when the bitter weather, the worst on record for 30 years, claimed the life of Sergeant Vincent Phillips. Separated in the darkness and driving snow, he died of exhaustion and hypothermia.

A day later, the larger group was only 10km (6 miles) from the Syrian border when they ran into a group of Iraqis. One man was wounded in the elbow and ankle and immobilized, while Swiss-born Trooper Robert Consiglio was killed. He died while providing covering fire with his FN Minimi light machine gun to allow the group to escape. Even so, two men were captured in this action.

Later, the two survivors swam across the icy, 400m (1312ft) wide Euphrates River. On the far side Lance Corporal 'Legs' Lane suffered from acute hypothermia and went into a coma. His companion, knowing that attempting to get help would mean his capture, approached local Iraqi civilians, but Cpl Lane died soon afterwards.

Corporal Ryan and his companion were now the only men still at liberty. As they were lying up in a small wadi, they saw a goatherd, and Ryan's companion decided to risk asking for help. A mistake: the man not only led the soldier straight to Iraqi forces, but also directed them back to where he had met the two SAS men.

Ryan was now exhausted and dehydrated. But his navigation, using only a compass, was impeccable. Over seven nights, he marched 188km (117 miles), dressed in only a lightweight desert uniform and with two packets of biscuits for nourishment, and little water.

On 30 January, Ryan crossed a barbed-wire fence and moved towards a town that was not 'blacked out' – suggesting that this was Syria. His first contact was with a goatherd, who took him home and gave him water, sweet tea and bread. Ryan broke down his M16, wrapping the parts in a plastic bag, to prove he was no threat.

He then made his way to the local police station, and eventually he was driven to Damascus, to the British Embassy. When he went to the Gulf, Ryan had weighed 82kg (182lb: 13 stone); now he was down to 63kg (140lb; 10 stone). It was two weeks before he could walk properly and six before any feeling returned to his fingers and toes.

CHAPTER 3

Conduct after Capture

Immediately following capture, a serviceman is disorientated and demoralized. He is now entirely at the mercy of his captors, but staying strong and alert remains essential to his mental and physical survival.

A captured soldier's first emotion can be a sense of failure, feeling that he has let down his unit and himself. However, although surrendering prisoners have been killed in the heat of battle, and the civil war in the former Yugoslavia saw mass executions of Muslim Croats by Serb Orthodox soldiers, his situation is not necessarily as bad he thinks it is – or certainly as it was in ancient times. Prisoners of war were then usually treated without mercy. Among the Greeks, for example, it was common practice to put to death the whole adult male population of a conquered state. The ancient Britons killed their prisoners in a barbarous fashion. The Ottoman Turks executed 30,000 Christian prisoners during the War of Candia in Crete (1667–1668). If prisoners were not killed, they might be blinded or have limbs amputated. The British two-fingered gesture of contempt dates back to the wars with medieval France, when captured English and Welsh archers had the index and second finger hacked off to prevent them ever pulling a bow. Archers would therefore taunt the French with this two-fingered gesture before a battle.

Where death or amputation was not inflicted, prisoners would be made slaves – some with talents or skills might, even in the ancient world, enjoy a comparatively good life. The practice of sparing and ransoming prisoners was

Left: A child soldier in Cambodia stands guard over a captured Khmer Rouge soldier in 1973. Bound and blindfolded, the prisoner has little chance of escape – however, there may be opportunities later.

Below: In an exercise in Nevada, two instructors from the US National Guard and United States Air Force play the role of downed F-18 crew as the crew of an HH-60 from the Naval Air Station at Coronado, California, interrogate and search them in a joint service exercise.

introduced in medieval western Europe. It was not a humanitarian impulse that drove this, but the opportunity to make vast fortunes. Fallen knights immobilized by the weight of their armour would be offered the chance to yield, or be killed by a long thin-bladed knife inserted through gaps in their armour.

In the 20th century, the Hague Conferences (1899 and 1907), the Geneva Convention in 1906 and the more detailed convention of 1929 provided international rules for the humane treatment of prisoners. A prisoner of war may not be treated as a criminal, but may be employed in non-military paid work. The prisoner has a right to adequate food, clothing and quarters and to the transmission of letters and parcels. A member of the armed forces is bound to supply name, rank and serial number, but cannot legally be compelled to give further information to the enemy. The provisions of the Geneva Convention of 1906 and 1929 were largely disregarded by totalitarian regimes, particularly those of Germany and Japan, during World War II.

Below: In an exercise in Nevada, two instructors from the US National Guard and United States Air Force play the role of downed F-18 crew as the crew of an HH-60 from the Naval Air Station at Coronado, California, interrogate and search them in a joint service exercise.

THE US MILITARY CODE OF CONDUCT

The Legal Behaviour Requirements for a US Military Member Held as a Prisoner of War.

ARTICLE I

I am an American, fighting in the forces which guard my country and our way of life. I am prepared to give my life in their defence.

ARTICLE II

I will never surrender of my own free will. If in command, I will never surrender the members of my command while they still have the means to resist.

ARTICLE III

If I am captured, I will continue to resist by all means available. I will make every effort to escape and to aid others to escape. I will accept neither parole nor special favours from the enemy.

ARTICLE IV

If I become a prisoner of war, I will keep faith with my fellow prisoners. I will give no information or take part in any action that might be harmful to my comrades. If I am senior, I will take command. If not, I will obey the lawful orders of those appointed over me and will back them up in every way.

ARTICLE V

When questioned, should I become a prisoner of war, I am required to give name, rank, service number, and date of birth. I will evade answering further questions to the utmost of my ability. I will make no oral or written statements disloyal to my country and its allies or harmful to their cause.

ARTICLE VI

I will never forget that I am an American, fighting for freedom, responsible for my actions, and dedicated to the principles which made my country free. I will trust in my God and in the United States of America.

POST-WWII POWS

After World War II, another Geneva Convention was convened in August 1949 to deal with the treatment of prisoners of war. The rules that were put forth there are binding on most of the countries of the world, although they have not always been strictly observed.

The Korean War saw the use of psychological warfare, or 'brainwashing' of prisoners, by North Korea. At the beginning of the war, the belligerents had promised to honour the principles of the 1949 convention. In spite of this, the communist forces were responsible for numerous violations: prisoners received inadequate food, clothing and shelter, and poor medical treatment, often resulting in loss of lives.

The US Military Code of Conduct (see feature box) was developed after the Korean War because of concern at the way that US PoWs had been manipulated by their communist captors.

In the course of truce negotiations during the Korean War, a new problem arose regarding repatriation of prisoners. Because of the apparent unwillingness of

Right: A detainee at Guantanamo Bay, Cuba, is escorted by US servicemen. His head is being held down so that he cannot observe the area. Coils of razor wire and handcuffs make escape from the base very difficult.

communist soldiers made prisoners of war to return to their homelands, the United Nations Command posited the principle of voluntary repatriation, stating that prisoners of war should not be returned against their will. Although the Geneva Convention does not specifically authorize voluntary repatriation, the United Nations Command held that the humanitarian spirit of the convention would be violated if the prisoners were forcibly repatriated. The new principle was finally incorporated in the armistice agreement on 26 July 1953 after a year-long deadlock; the agreement granted belligerents the right to speak with prisoners opposed to repatriation.

During the Vietnam War, captured US pilots were used for propaganda in the same way that the Chinese and North Koreans had manipulated prisoners. Now, the advent of satellite television meant that pictures of prisoners can be beamed around the world almost minutes after their capture.

WHO IS A PRISONER OF WAR?

On 28 January 2002, the US government announced that fighters who had been taken prisoner during operations against Islamic militants in Afghanistan were to be classified as 'unlawful combatants'. US President George W. Bush made it clear that prisoners captured in Afghanistan – and those who were being held in the US base at Guantanamo Bay in Cuba – would not be treated as prisoners of war.

A US Army pamphlet on the law of war provides this definition: 'An unlawful combatant is an individual who is not authorized to take a direct part in hostilities but does. [...] Unlawful combatants are a proper object of attack while engaging as combatants. [...] If captured, they may be tried and punished.' As examples, the pamphlet mentions civilians who engage in war without authorization; non-combat members of the military, such as medics or chaplains, who engage in combat; and soldiers who fight out of uniform. In World War II, the United States captured eight German saboteurs dressed in civilian clothes and executed six of them. However, under the Geneva Conventions, it's up to an independent judge to determine the status of the 'detainees', and not to whoever detains them. In addition, Canadian regulations on prisoner-of-war status dictate that detainees must be brought before a military tribunal to determine whether they're prisoners of war or not.

After weeks of international criticism in 2002, the White House spokesman, Ari Fleischer, said there would be no change in the way the fighters were treated.

The row over whether the Guantanamo Bay detainees qualified for the special provisions afforded to prisoners of war (PoWs) centred around the Geneva Conventions on the rights of prisoners.

The key principles grew out of an original agreement dating back to 1864.

They are established in one of four conventions adopted in 1949 and ratified by 189 countries. A later set of rules, the 'Additional Protocol' was drafted in 1977 (see box). It significantly alters the criteria of eligibility for PoW status, but neither the US or Afghanistan are among the 159 signatories.

ADDITIONAL PROTOCOL

According to Article 43 of Additional Protocol I, 'any combatant...who falls into the power of an adverse party shall be a prisoner of war'. Article 44 then clarifies the definition of the term 'combatant'.

According to paragraph 2, while all combatants are obliged to comply with the laws of war, violations of these rules 'shall not deprive a combatant of his right to be a combatant or [...] to be a prisoner of war'. The only exceptions to this are in relation to the use of clothing and symbols to make combatants identifiable. Paragraph 3 recognizes that it is not always possible for combatants to distinguish themselves from the civilian population, as they are obliged to do under international law. It states that a fighter 'shall retain his status as a combatant, provided that, in such situations, he carries his arms openly', during each military engagement and while visible to the adversary as he prepares to attack.

According to paragraph 4, if he fails to do this, he forfeits his status as a POW, but 'shall, nevertheless, be given protections equivalent in all respects to those accorded to prisoners of war'.

The relevant sections of both documents are summarized below:

Geneva Convention (III)

According to Article 4 of the third Geneva Convention, PoWs include individuals in the following categories who have fallen into the power of the enemy:

Members of the armed forces of a party to the conflict, or of militias or volunteer corps forming part of such armed forces.

Members of other militias and members of other volunteer corps, including those of organized resistance movements.

Members of regular armed forces who profess allegiance to a government or an authority not recognized by the detaining power.

Inhabitants of a non-occupied territory who have spontaneously taken up arms to resist an invading force, provided that they carry arms openly and respect the laws and customs of war.

Article 5 of the convention states that, 'should any doubt arise' as to whether detainees fit these categories, they 'shall enjoy the protection of the present convention' until 'their status has been determined by a competent tribunal'.

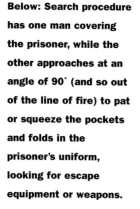

Below: Search procedure has one man covering the prisoner, while the other approaches at an angle of 90˚ (and so out of the line of fire) to pat or squeeze the pockets and folds in the prisoner's uniform, looking for escape equipment or weapons.

There are various precedents for interpreting the Geneva Convention in practical situations. Viet Cong fighters captured during the Vietnam War were eventually given PoW status, despite the fact that they wore nondescript black clothing with no insignia. During the Korean War, although the US did not recognize the Chinese regime diplomatically, it still treated Chinese captives from the Korean War as PoWs. While it could be asserted that both the Luftwaffe and RAF broke the rules of war by attacking civilian targets during World War II, this did not exclude all captured aircrew from PoW status.

Some legal experts have suggested that a distinction should be made between al-Qaeda and Taleban prisoners, as the Taleban were the military force of the de facto government of Afghanistan – even though it was recognized by only three governments – while al-Qaeda are a stateless militia.

Above: A US pilot is escorted by his 'captors' during a survival, evasion and escape exercise. Though exercises can never duplicate the full trauma of capture, they can acquaint 'prone to capture' personnel with important elements.

THE SHOCK OF CAPTURE

Being captured by an enemy is a severe psychological shock, even for veteran soldiers. Only those who have experienced such an event can appreciate the desire to talk to captors, sometimes without being able to stop. A soldier must steel himself from the very first moment of captivity to say as little as possible. Under the Geneva Convention, he is expected to give his name, rank, number and date of birth (this allows the Red Cross hopefully to keep track of his movements and health condition, as well as to notify his next of kin that he has survived), but he should resist the desire to say anything else.

After capture, most soldiers adopt one of two attitudes. They either try to appeal to their captors by smiles and other friendly gestures, or they show defiance by scowling, cursing or exhibiting signs of aggression. They should do neither. The co-operative prisoner will actually make his life more difficult because his captors

EIGHT CHARACTERS

The CIA has identified eight character types that emerge in the setting of interrogation.

1) **The orderly-obstinate character**
2) **The optimistic character.** This respond best to a kindly, parental approach. If withholding, they can often be handled effectively by the Mutt-and-Jeff technique discussed later (see page 76). Pressure tactics or hostility will make them retreat inside themselves, whereas reassurance will bring them out. They tend to seek promises, to cast the interrogator in the role of protector and problem-solver.
3) **The greedy, demanding character.** This kind of person affixes himself to others like a leech and clings obsessively. Although extremely dependent and passive, he constantly demands that others take care of him and gratify his wishes.
4) **The anxious, self-centred character.** Although this person is fearful, he is engaged in a constant struggle to conceal his fears. He is frequently a daredevil who compensates for his anxiety by pretending that there is no such thing as danger.
5) **The guilt-ridden character.** This kind of person has a strong, cruel, unrealistic

Above: An exercise at a Code of Conduct training base in Hawaii replicates the aggressive interrogation techniques used by the North Koreans. The 'prisoner' has been accused of spying.

conscience. His whole life seems devoted to reliving his feelings of guilt. Sometimes he seems determined to atone; at other times he insists that whatever went wrong is the fault of somebody else.

6) **The schizoid or strange character** lives in a world of fantasy much of the time. Sometimes he seems unable to distinguish reality from the realm of his own creating.
7) **The exception** believes that the world owes him a great deal. He feels that he suffered a gross injustice, usually early in life, and should be repaid.
8) **The average or normal character.**

Left: Reality – an elderly man detained by soldiers of the US Army 2/87 Infantry Division in April, 2004 at Ghanzi, Afghanistan. His hands are secured with plastic handcuffs and a label attached giving the location in which he was captured. The image was deleted by the US Army because of sensitivity about the detainee procedure, but later recovered using disk recovery software.

will see him as a useful subject for interrogation and return to question him. Interrogators will use a variety of ploys to identify those who are high-value prisoners that merit further questioning. If the officer or NCO has removed obvious insignia and joined the anonymous mass of prisoners, an interrogator will shout out orders to the group and watch to see if they look for guidance from someone in authority within the group.

High-value prisoners need not be from the senior ranks. An officer's driver will have overheard conversations or his radio operator will have a shrewd idea of future plans. Interrogators are trained manipulators, and they are skilled in easing information from unsuspecting soldiers. What may start as iron-clad resolve may disappear quickly after several days of hiding from the enemy.

Immediately following capture, prisoners will be disarmed and searched for anything of intelligence value – this will also help interrogators to place the rank or role of their captive. The escorts for PoWs should not fraternize with their charges, who may be hooded to prevent them identifying reference points or enemy equipment or dispositions.

The prisoners will be moved to the rear and may eventually find themselves in a formally structured PoW camp. Under the 1949 Geneva Convention, a prisoners' representative, normally the most senior officer or NCO in the camp, should be appointed to provide an interface with the camp authorities, who in the words of the Convention are the 'Detaining Power'. The representative has the responsibility of looking after the prisoners' physical, spiritual and intellectual wellbeing. This will include messing and the distribution of Red Cross parcels, letters and news, counselling and grievances. It is essential for the PoWs that they do not give up hope or, even worse, start internal squabbles and lose any sense of loyalty or cohesion.

During the Vietnam War, captured US pilots reported that after the abortive US Special Forces raid on a suspected North Vietnamese PoW camp at Son Tay on the night of 20–21 November 1970, the North Vietnamese, fearing a repeat performance but not knowing when and where, closed the outlying PoW camps and consolidated all PoWs in the two main prisons in downtown Hanoi. These were the former French prisons of Halo and Culac. The number of PoWs at these two prisons now grew to the extent that PoWs lived in groups, rather than what for many had been solitary confinement. Morale immediately improved and, as a result, general health improved with it. Some PoWs have stated that lives were saved by the move. Mail delivery and food both improved substantially. One veteran of these new enlarged PoW camps remembered a fellow pilot who as a student had worked as a cinema usher. The PoW pilot had a remarkable recall of the many films he had seen while working and, as his fellow pilots sat silently with eyes closed, he would paint a word picture of the films, characters and plots.

Right: A North Vietnamese nurse gives first aid to a US pilot shot down in 1970, while an NVA soldier stands guard in the background. Ejecting from a combat aircraft can cause injuries that can prevent escape and evasion.

THE SON TAY RAID

On 20–21 November 1970, a joint force composed of USAF Special Operations and rescue personnel and US Army Special Forces, supported by US Navy Carrier Task Force 77, made a daring raid on the Son Tay prison camp located less than 48km (30 miles) from Hanoi, North Vietnam. The objective was to rescue as many as 100 US captives thought to be held there. The assault troops, in six ARRS helicopters accompanied by two C-130 aircraft, flew 643km (400 miles) to Son Tay from bases in Thailand. US Navy pilots made a diversionary raid while 116 USAF and Navy aircraft from seven air bases and three aircraft carriers flew refuelling, surface-to-air missile suppression, fighter cover, close air support, early warning, communications support and reconnaissance missions. Although no prisoners were found in camp, the raid was a brilliant success in transporting, landing and recovering an assault force of 92 USAF and 56 Army personnel without the loss of a single man.

Although no prisoners were rescued, the raid focused world attention on the plight of the PoWs, raised their morale and resulted in improved living conditions for all U.S. prisoners of the North Vietnamese. The men of the Joint Task Force earned the admiration of their countrymen for risking their lives in an attempt to bring freedom to others.

INTERROGATIONS

Interrogations can be divided into tactical and long term. Tactical interrogations are conducted soon after capture and are intended to gain short-term intelligence that is probably valuable for the next 24 hours. The interrogator will want to know about unit positions, minefields or ambush sites. He will be keen to take advantage of the initial 'shock of capture' to elicit information.

Long-term interrogation may be conducted at the PoW camp in a dedicated interrogation centre where the prisoner may be held in solitary confinement. During this process, a detailed record of his answers is built up. In these conditions, the interrogators may use techniques like sleep deprivation to confuse the prisoner, meals may be served at random times, and the lights switched on and off in the cell to suggest the passage of day and night. He may be held in cramped conditions in which he cannot lie down.

The detainees may be stripped and humiliated by being paraded in front of women. Hooding and masking along with loose clothing and 'white noise' – taped sound that resembles hissing air – may be employed to induce sensory deprivation and confusion. Long-term interrogation may be used to build up a picture of enemy strategy and the way in which a campaign will be conducted. The war against terrorism has highlighted the value of long-term intelligence as interrogators try to build up a picture of terrorist organizations and strategies.

**Right: A member of a
'guerrilla' force stands
guard over hooded
evaders during a joint-
service escape and
evasion exercise held in
1987 at Outlying Field,
Choctaw, United States.
In all exercises, there is
an element of unreality
– the 'enemy' will never
kill their captives.**

Before he or she begins work, an interrogator will be given an Information Requirement (IR). The IR is the information that intelligence officers wish to know about. Corporal Hans Scharff, a Luftwaffe interrogator of WWII, developed a technique that was so low-key and unconfrontational that captured USAAF aircrew thought that they were enjoying a conversation about their squadron and its personalities. Scharff had built up detailed files on the USAAF squadrons and was using the 'We know all' technique of interrogation – the pilots chatted away freely because they did not realize that within the conversation he had concealed his IR. The USAAF prisoner would provide the information because the way in which the question had been posed seemed completely innocuous.

A military interrogation differs from one conducted by a law officer. The former is looking for information, the latter for an admission of guilt and confession. In some regimes, a military detainee may be seen as a valuable resource to be exploited for propaganda. The video-taped 'confession' to crimes or illegal acts may be extracted after a mixture of psychological and physical coercion. Even if the confession looks contrived to informed observers, it may still be effective for less sophisticated domestic TV audiences.

FIFTEEN PLOYS

Interrogators have 15 ploys or techniques for questioning.

1) Direct or Friendly Logical: Asking straightforward questions. This is often the starting point for more specialized techniques. For some PoWs still in the shock of capture, this can be very effective.

2) Incentive/Removal of Incentive: Providing a reward or removing a privilege, above and beyond those that are required by the Geneva Convention from detainees. These can be quite small rewards that take on greater significance in the context of an interrogation or PoW camp – a cigarette for a smoker, for example.

3) Emotional Love: Playing on the love or loyalty a detainee has for an individual or a group. Among the prisoner's possessions may be photographs of spouses and children and letters may also give names and home locations. Group loyalty may be to the regiment or region – the prisoner may be told that his regiment has been abandoned by other formations.

4) Emotional Hate: Playing on the hatred a detainee has for an individual or group. The prisoner may feel that he or his group has been let down by higher command or that elite units despise his corps or formation.

5) Fear Up Harsh: Significantly increasing the fear level in a detainee.

6) Fear Up Mild: Moderately increasing the fear level.

7) Reduced Fear: Reducing the level of fear in a detainee.

8) Pride and Ego Up: Boosting the ego and self-esteem of a detainee. A significant technique when the prisoner may feel ashamed that he surrendered or that as an officer or NCO he is superior to the enlisted personnel.

9) Pride and Ego Down: Attacking or insulting the ego of a detainee, not beyond the limits that would apply to a PoW. This has included stripping, searching and forcible shaving of facial hair.

Left: With the captive seated on a stool, an interrogator – anonymous in civilian clothes – uses a 'fear up mild' approach. With an insecure prisoner, this may produce fear and cooperation; if not, other, more aggressive, techniques are available.

10) Futility: Invoking a feeling of futility in the detainee. This is the 'What's the point' attitude that can be felt by reluctant conscript soldiers – particularly if they have seen friends killed in a fruitless operation.

11) We Know All: Convincing the detainee that the interrogator knows all about the detainee's background and the answers to the questions he is asking. This can be built up from information collected from other prisoners from the same unit or formation. Sometimes quite trifling information like the name of a senior officer's dog can trigger a feeling in the prisoner that there are no secrets.

12) Establish Your Identity: Convincing the detainee that the interrogator has mistaken the detainee for someone else. Underlying this is inducing in the prisoner the fear that he may be punished for a crime for which he is not guilty. A variant on this is for the interrogator to act as if he is rather stupid and consequently produce a slight contempt in the prisoner.

13) Repetition: Continuously repeating the same question to the detainee within interrogation periods of normal duration. It can be as boring for the questioner as the prisoner, but can eventually cause him to crack.

14) File and Dossier. Convincing the detainee that the interrogator has a damning but inaccurate file that, in the detainees interest, should be corrected.

15) Mutt and Jeff: A team consisting of a friendly and a harsh interrogator. The harsh interrogator might employ the Fear Up techniques and the friendly the Pride and Ego. The friendly one may introduce himself to the detainee by apologizing for the behaviour of his colleague and explaining that his behaviour was unacceptable.

COERCION AND TORTURE

The threat of coercion usually weakens or destroys resistance more effectively than coercion itself. The threat to inflict pain, for example, can trigger fears more damaging than the immediate sensation of pain. In fact, most people underestimate their capacity to withstand pain. The same principle holds for other fears: sustained long enough, a strong fear of anything vague or unknown induces regression.

Some coercive techniques have been developed that leave no external marks on a detainee. In the so-called 'Water Cure', the subject is tied or held down in a chair, with his face forced back and covered with a cloth, and water is then poured over the cloth. The subject feels like he is drowning and this is done to encourage the subject to talk. Another variation is to pour water down the throat of the subject or to immerse him in a bath face downwards, the interrogators taking care not to drown the subject, but to make him feel the sensation of drowning.

Electric torture has included cattle goads as well as the hand-crank generator for field telephones and radios. Terminals are connected to genitalia or inserted into the mouth or nose and the current switched on for about three minutes. Sometimes a

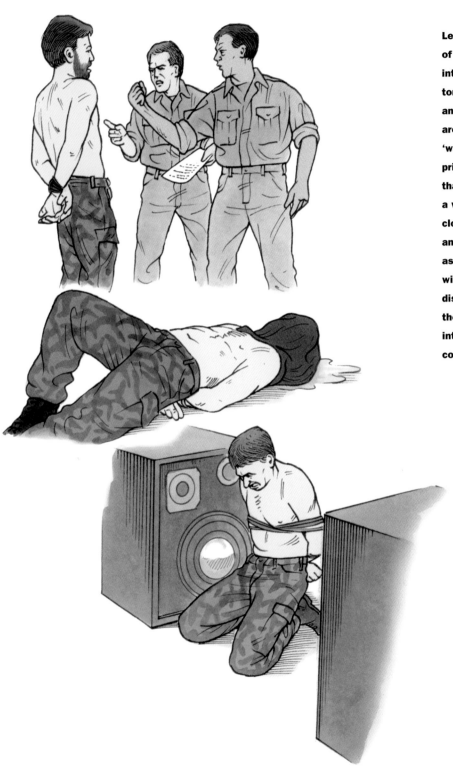

Left: The techniques of 'fear up harsh' interrogation merge into torture when threats and aggressive demands are followed up. The 'water cure' gives the prisoner the sensation that he is drowning as a water-soaked cloth closes over his mouth and nose. Loud noise as music or 'white noise' will deafen and disorientate him so that the next (music-free) interrogation actually comes as a relief.

doctor is present to check that the torture will not kill the detainee. Simple beatings may be used – by focusing on areas like the soles of the feet, pain can be inflicted without leaving obvious marks. This can be significant if a video 'confession' is required, and facial bruising needs to be avoided. Detainees may be tied up and lifted off the ground so that their weight bears on their arms or legs. A variant of this torture technique is to hang the victim upside down over a smoky fire.

Other techniques include requiring the detainee to run around a heated room while wearing warm clothes or permitting him to wear only underwear while holding him in a cell with a sharp stone floor, concrete bench and no lavatory. In Korea. prisoners found that the temperature sunk so low that they could not sit or lie down. Another cruel practice involves forcing the detainee to sit on a stool with his hands hanging loosely by his side and feet stretched out. He is kept in this position for around 180 hours until the his feet swell so painfully that he is unable to walk.

The effectiveness of a threat of physical violence depends not only on the character of the detainee and whether he believes that his questioner can and will carry out the threat, but also on the interrogator's reasons for threatening. If the interrogator threatens because he is angry, the detainee frequently senses the fear of failure underlying the anger and is strengthened in his own resolve to resist. Threats delivered coldly are more effective than those shouted in rage. It is especially important for an interrogator that a threat not be uttered in response to the detainee's own expressions of hostility. If such expressions are ignored, this can induce feelings of guilt inthe captive, whereas retorts in kind relieve his feelings.

Right: Hooding can disorientate a prisoner. However, if he has been through 'Conduct after Capture' training, he will know how much can be picked up through hearing, smell and the paths and corridors along which he is marched. If his captors talk, he can work out their number and who is in command.

PSYCHOLOGICAL PRESSURE

During the show trials in Stalin's Soviet Union in the 1930s, committed communists were induced to confess publicly to crimes against the state. One man recalled that as his NKVD gaolers led him through the corridors of a prison, they showed him a man undergoing a brutal and painful interrogation. The room was blood spattered and the man was screaming, protesting his innocence – the NKVD officers asked their new captive, 'Do you want to go through that and then confess, or just get it over with and confess?' The man confessed even though the charges were completely false.

The use of pain and fear can be counter-productive. A frightened detainee may say anything to stop the torture and this information may not be accurate, but rather what he thinks his interrogator wants to hear.

TRIUMPH

When an interrogator senses that the subject's resistance is wavering, that his desire to yield is growing stronger than his wish to continue his resistance, the CIA asserts that the time has come to provide him with the acceptable rationalization: a face-saving reason or excuse for compliance.

Novice interrogators may be tempted to seize upon the initial yielding triumphantly and to personalize the victory. Such a temptation must be rejected immediately. An interrogation is not a game played by two people, one to become the winner and the other the loser. It is simply a method of obtaining correct and useful information. Therefore the interrogator will aim to intensify the subject's desire to cease struggling by showing him how he can do so without seeming to abandon principle, self-protection or other initial causes of resistance. If, instead of providing the right rationalization at the right time, the interrogator seizes upon the subject's wavering in a gloating manner, opposition will stiffen again.

Experienced interrogators will be able to read their subject's reactions and behaviour and pass this information on to the next man tasked with interrogating the captive. They will recommend an approach – like Repetition or Pride Up.

At the close of the interrogation, they will leave the detainee with a 'bridge' – something for him to worry about while he is alone. The bridge may be the suggestion that the next interrogator uses brutal methods, or that letters from home for the detainee have arrived and will be handed over to him at the next meeting.

The best strategy for a detainee to take during interrogation is simply not to give any information beyond name, rank, service number and date of birth – the 'Big Four'. Any other information may be exploited and used as a lever against the

SOLITARY CONFINEMENT

Aircrew who have been shot down deep inside enemy territory may initially be held in solitary confinement. Their captors will wish to gain information about forthcoming air operations, weapons and tactics. They may also see them as a possible tool in a wider psychological campaign if they can be induced to appear on television and denounce their country and the war.

In order to break down their resistance, they may be held in solitary confinement. The effects of confinement have been identified by the CIA as:

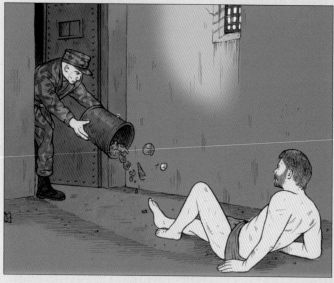

Above: As an act of humiliation, a guard throws a crude meal into the cell of a near naked prisoner. Survival in solitary confinement requires a strong will or deep political or religious convictions to maintain the prisoner's ability to endure.

1) The more completely the place of confinement eliminates sensory stimuli, the more rapidly and deeply will the interrogatee be affected. Results produced only after weeks or months of imprisonment in an ordinary cell can be duplicated in hours or days in a cell which has no light (or weak artificial light that never varies), which is sound-proofed, and in which familiar smells are eliminated. An environment still more subject to control, such as a water-tank or iron lung, is even more effective.

2) An early effect of such an environment is anxiety. How soon it appears and how strong it is depends upon the psychological characteristics of the individual.

3) The interrogator can benefit from the subject's anxiety. As the interrogator becomes linked in the subject's mind with the reward of lessened anxiety, human contact and meaningful activity – and thus with providing relief for growing discomfort – the questioner assumes a benevolent role.

4) The deprivation of stimuli induces regression by depriving the subject's mind of contact with an outer world and thus forcing it in upon itself. At the same time, the calculated provision of stimuli during interrogation tends to make the regressed subject view the interrogator as a father-figure. The result, normally, is a strengthening of the subject's tendencies toward compliance.

detainee or other prisoners. To questions that go beyond the Big Four, the reply should be 'I cannot answer that question, sir'. He should not prefix the reply with 'I'm sorry'. If the interrogation is being videoed, his captors can splice together a 'confession' in which the detainee appears to apologize for some criminal act.

He should beware of the 'Red Cross Official', an enemy interrogator in disguise who requests that he sign documents or receipts. This signature may then be attached to a fake confession and this, in turn, used to blackmail or pressure the detainee. He should not give the interrogator anything to key on, such as being thirsty, hungry or how long it has been since he heard from his spouse or family. He should give careful short answers to questions and, if there is a cover story, keep it as simple as possible. The interrogators will be keeping a record of the detainee's replies and will check them before the next encounter. The detainee should try to show no emotion through facial expressions or body language.

From the moment of capture, the serviceman must aim to attract as little attention from his captors or jailers as possible. He must become the 'grey man'. This will prevent him from being singled out for interrogation, when he will be under closer guard, and will greatly help his chances of escape.

To play the grey man, he should stand or sit motionless with head slightly bowed. He should avoid eye contact, but if forced to look at the enemy, he should focus on his interrogator's forehead or bridge of the nose. This gives the impression that he is making eye contact, but reduces the chance that he may show emotion by an eye reaction. He should speak only if spoken to.

If the interrogators use physical violence or torture, the detainee should not remain silent – cries of pain and whimpering will mislead his tormentors into believing they have genuinely inflicted pain, and so reduce the risk of real injury. The detainee will have scored a small victory in his mind if he convinces his questioners that they have caused him pain.

If he comes under a concerted attack, the detainee should try to fall to the ground and manoeuvre himself into a corner – this will reduce the number of people who can strike him and the attackers will hinder one another. If the detainee can roll onto his stomach, he will protect most of his vital organs. He should pull in his chin and try to keep his elbows close to his body to protect his kidneys.

Under brutal or sustained interrogation, a prisoner of war will have to dig deep into his reserves of moral courage. He should always reassure himself that his tormentors cannot read his mind.

Above: A British military policeman from 160 Provost Company, 5th Airborne Brigade, during a prisoner handling training exercise. The soldier playing the part of 'captured enemy personnel' (CEP) has been restrained with plasticuffs.

CHAPTER 4

Escaping Captivity

The best moment for a captive soldier to attempt to escape is immediately after he has been captured. He will probably be in his best physical condition at that time and will be familiar with the terrain in which he has been taken prisoner.

Prison camp rations will be usually barely enough to sustain life, and certainly not enough to build up a reserve of energy. The physical treatment, poor medical care and rations of prison life quickly cause physical weakness, night blindness and loss of coordination and reasoning power.

EARLY ESCAPE

The following are reasons for making an early escape:

- Friendly fire or air strikes may cause enough confusion and disorder to provide a chance of escape.
- The first troops assigned to escorting prisoners will probably not be as well trained in handling prisoners as guards in the echelon area. Some may even be walking wounded who are distracted by their own condition. These soldiers will probably not have the interest, the time or the training in handling PoWs.
- The longer the soldier remains in captivity, the greater is his chance of being sent to a secure PoW camp with guards specially trained in preventing escapes.
- The would-be escaper will probably know something about the area where he has been captured and may know the locations of nearby friendly units.

Left: An Iranian prisoner of war despairs near the barbed wire perimeter of a PoW camp near Ranado, Iraq, in October 1983. He was captured during the Iran–Iraq war over border disputes, which lasted from 1980 to 1988.

Right: Even with the support of companions, prison life can depress morale, and boredom must be combated with games and conversation. It is essential to sustain the will to survive.

- The way the soldier escapes depends on what he can think of to fit the situation. The only general rules are to escape early and escape when the enemy is distracted. The prisoners may contrive an 'incident' to distract the guards – a fight or the collapse of one of their number. Air strikes or artillery fire may force prisoners and guards to take cover and allow prisoners to slip away.
- The longer the soldier remains in captivity, the more thoroughly he will be searched and the further he will be sent behind enemy lines. Once incarcerated in a purpose-built PoW camp, the rules of escape and evasion will change drastically.

POW HEALTH

In either in a PoW camp or during escape and evasion, cleanliness is an important factor in preventing infection and disease. Poor hygiene can reduce the prisoner's chances of survival let alone escape.

A daily shower with hot water and soap is ideal, but the captive can stay clean without this luxury. He should use a cloth and soapy water to wash himself, paying special attention to the feet, armpits, crotch, hands and hair, as these are prime areas for infestation and infection. If water is scarce, he can take an 'air' bath. He should remove as much of his clothing as practical and expose his body to the sun and air for at least one hour, taking care not to sunburn.

Germs on a prisoner's hands can infect food and wounds. He should wash his hands after handling any material that is likely to carry germs, after visiting the latrine, after caring for the sick, and before handling any food, food utensils or drinking water. Fingernails should be kept closely trimmed and clean.

Hair can become a haven for bacteria or fleas, lice and other parasites. Keeping hair clean, combed and trimmed helps to avoid this danger. The prisoner should thoroughly clean his mouth and teeth with a toothbrush at least once each day. If he does not have a toothbrush, he can adopt an old African technique and can make a chewing stick. He should find a twig about 20cm (8in) long and 1cm (0.4in) wide. He chews one end of the stick to separate the fibres and then brushes his teeth thoroughly. Another way is to wrap a clean strip of cloth around his fingers and rub the teeth with it to wipe away food particles. He can also brush his teeth with small amounts of sand, baking soda, salt or soap. He should then rinse his mouth out with water, salt water or willow bark tea. Flossing his teeth with string or fibre helps oral hygiene.

If he develops cavities, he can make temporary fillings by placing candle wax, tobacco, aspirin, hot pepper, toothpaste or powder, or portions of a ginger root into the cavity. Prior to this, he should make sure the cavity is clean by rinsing or picking the particles out.

The prisoner should also pay close attention to the condition of his feet. Boots and shoes should be broken in before the soldier wears them on any mission. He should wash and massage his feet daily and trim his toenails straight across. The

MAKING SOAP

If the prisoner does not have soap, he can use ashes or sand; or if circumstances allow, he can make soap from animal fat and wood ashes. To make soap:

1) Extract grease from animal fat by cutting the fat into small pieces and cooking them in a pot.

2) Add enough water to the pot to keep the fat from sticking as it cooks. Cook the fat slowly, stirring frequently.

3) After the fat is rendered, pour the grease into a container to harden.

4) Place ashes in a container with a spout near the bottom.

5) Pour water over the ashes and collect the liquid that drips out of the spout in a separate container. This liquid is the potash, or lye. Another way to get the lye is to pour the slurry (the mixture of ashes and water) through a straining cloth.

6) In a cooking pot, mix two parts grease to one part potash.

7) Place this mixture over a fire and boil it until it thickens.

8) After the mixture – the soap – cools, it can be used in the semi-liquid state directly from the pot or can be poured into a pan, allowed to harden, and cut it into bars for later use.

soldier should wear an insole and the proper size of dry socks, and powder and check his feet daily for blisters. As a prisoner, he may not have access to insoles, but a simple expedient is to tear several sheets of newspaper to the size of his boot and fit them inside. When he changes his socks, he should use the top of the sock to clean between his toes.

If he develops a small blister, he should not puncture it, as an intact blister is safe from infection. He should apply a padding material around the blister to relieve pressure and reduce friction and use the following blister first aid:

• If the blister bursts, treat it as an open wound.
• Clean and dress it daily and pad around it.
• Leave large blisters intact.

To avoid having the blister burst or tear under pressure and cause a painful and open sore, do the following: Obtain a sewing-type needle and a clean or sterilized thread. Run the needle and thread through the blister after cleaning it. Detach the needle and leave both ends of the thread hanging out of the blister. The thread will absorb the liquid inside. This reduces the size of the hole and ensures that the hole does not close up. Pad around the blister.

If the prisoner is planning an escape, he will need to build up his strength and stamina, but he will also require a certain amount of rest to keep going in the attempt. If possible, he should plan for regular rest periods of at least 10 minutes per hour during his daily routine. He must learn to make himself comfortable under less than ideal conditions. A change from mental to physical activity or vice versa can be refreshing when time or situation does not permit total relaxation.

The prisoner should keep clothing and bedding as clean as possible to reduce the chance of skin infection as well as to decrease the danger of parasitic infestation. He cleans outer clothing whenever it becomes soiled. If possible, he wears clean underclothing and socks each day. If water is scarce, the prisoner should 'air clean' his clothing by shaking, airing and sunning it for two hours. If he is using a sleeping bag, he turns it inside out after each use, fluffs it and airs it. If lice infest clothing, an old Russian Army trick from World War II is to bury each article of clothing under the ground with just one corner left above the ground. The lice collect there and can be burned off with a candle flame.

ESCAPE FROM A CAMP

Escape from a purpose-made PoW camp is hard, but not impossible. The prisoners will be able to build up a picture of the behaviour of the guards and their routine. They will know who is diligent and who is lazy, and will also study patrol routes and when the day or night shift take over.

In World War II, in camps where the soil was sandy, prisoners tried tunnelling. With modern seismic intruder alarm systems that can pick up the vibrations from a walking man, this option is less viable. However, if the camp is rudimentary there may be opportunities to slip under a fence or remove part of it. Passive night-vision equipment also makes movement by night less effective.

Often the best way out is the way the PoW entered the camp – through the gate. Prisoners have disguised themselves as guards or civilians employed in the camp, and simply walked out. Vans, trucks or trailers used for transporting

Left: Even the simplest tools like spoons or, better still, knives can assist escape. In a poorly built prison, there may be scope to weaken brick walls to give access to areas from which it is easier to escape.

laundry, rations or rubbish can present an opportunity. However, most of these techniques require support from fellow prisoners to distract or delay the guards while the escaper makes his move. Prisoners will also assist one another with collecting items that can be used as tools and which may assist in escaping and evading. History has shown that not every prisoner has the drive to escape, but may still be keen to help those who wish to.

Many escape plans have used rivers as a means of escape. A small boat is ideal, but even empty water containers can provide flotation. As long as the fugitive uses the camouflage of the riverbank and avoids the natural hazards of the river, he may be able to reach friendly territory. However, rivers often have fishermen who are intimately familiar with their patch and who will notice unusual boats or flotsam.

Darkness and bad weather may make the going tough for the escaper, but these conditions will also mean that guards and search teams are not at their most alert.

MEET THE PEOPLE

Before he attempts to escape the PoW camp, the escaper must address whether he will attempt to pass himself off as a local or concentrate on evasion. Generally speaking, it is better for the escaper if he does not try to look like a local. He may not speak the language, have the coloration or build.

In some areas, the population need not be hostile, but the soldier now on the run must give serious consideration to dealing with the local people. Do they have a primitive culture? Are they farmers, fishermen, friendly people, or enemy? As a survivor, effective cross-cultural communication can vary radically from area to area and from people to people. It may mean interaction with people of an extremely primitive culture or contact with people who have a relatively modern culture.

A culture is identified by standards of behaviour that its members consider proper and acceptable, but these may not conform to an outsider's idea of what is normal. No matter who the people are, the survivor/evader can expect that they

Right: Theory – crossing a wire mesh fence topped with coiled barbed wire is possible if the mesh is wide enough to serve as a foothold. Wrapping a blanket over the barbed wire prevents it snagging.

Above: Practice – razor
wire and barbed wire
tops a fence made of
steel mesh panels. The
razor wire overhangs the
fence, so climbing, even
with the assistance of a
ladder, would be very
difficult.

will have laws, social and economic values, and political and religious beliefs that may be radically different from his. Before deploying into his area of operations, he should study these different cultural aspects. Prior study and preparation will help him make or avoid contact if he has to deal with the local population.

People may be friendly, unfriendly, or they may simply choose to ignore him. Their attitude might be unknown. If the people are known to be friendly, he should try to keep them friendly through courtesy and respect for their religion, politics, social customs, habits and all other aspects of their culture. If the people are known to be enemies or are unknowns, he should make every effort to avoid any contact and leave no sign of his presence.

If, after careful observation, he can determine that an unknown people are friendly, he may contact them if he absolutely needs their help. Usually, he has little to fear and much to gain from cautious, respectful contact with local people of friendly or neutral countries. If he displays common decency and, most importantly, shows respect for their customs, he should be able to avoid trouble and even get help. To make contact, the soldier should wait until only one person is near and, if possible, let that person make the initial approach. Most people will be willing to help a survivor in need. However, local political attitudes, instruction or propaganda efforts may change the attitudes of otherwise friendly people. Conversely, in unfriendly countries, many people, especially in remote areas, may feel animosity toward their politicians and may be friendlier toward a survivor.

Right: One method of escape is to disguise oneself as the civilian staff who work around the PoW camp. This is effective where captors and captives are from the same ethnic group and where captives have enough time to make disguises.

BE FRIENDLY

The key to successful contact with local peoples is to be friendly, courteous and patient. Displaying fear, showing weapons, and making sudden or threatening movements can frighten a local person. Such actions can in turn prompt a hostile response. When attempting a contact, the soldier should smile as often as possible. Many local peoples are shy and seem unapproachable, or they may ignore him. He should approach them slowly and not rush his contact.

If the fugitive does not speak the local language, using sign language or acting out needs or questions can be effective. Many people are used to such language and communicate using non-verbal signs. However, the soldier should try to learn a few words and phrases of the local language in and around the area of operations, even if this is as simple as 'Yes', 'No' and 'Hello'. Trying to speak someone's language is one of the best ways to show respect for his culture. Since English is a widely used language, some of the local people may understand a few words.

In some simpler cultures, certain behaviours or practices may be taboo. These range from moving through religious or sacred places to prohibitions against killing certain animals. The survivor/evader should learn the rules and follow them, watching and learning as much as possible. Such actions will help to strengthen relations and provide new knowledge and skills that may be very important later. He can seek advice on local hazards and find out from friendly people where the hostile people are. The survivor/evader should always remember that people often insist that other peoples are hostile, simply because they do not understand different cultures and distant peoples.

Frequently, local peoples in the developing world will suffer from contagious diseases. The survivor/evader should build a separate shelter, if possible, and avoid physical contact without giving the impression of doing so. He should personally prepare his food and drink, if he can do so without giving offence. Frequently, the local people will accept the use of 'personal or religious custom' as an explanation for isolationist behaviour. In addition, many people consider touching taboo and such actions may be dangerous. Any sexual contact should be avoided for both health and social reasons.

Exceptional hospitality can be a strong cultural trait among some people, and they may seriously reduce their own supplies to feed a stranger. Accept what they offer and share it equally with all present. Eat in the same way they eat and, most important, try to eat all they offer. The soldier should keep any promises he makes, because other escapees may follow and reap the benefits – or not. He should make some kind of payment for food, supplies and so forth and respect the locals' privacy, never entering a house unless invited.

The survivor/evader should remember that in today's world of fast-paced international politics, political attitudes and commitments within nations can change rapidly. The population of many countries, especially politically hostile countries, must not be considered friendly just because the people do not demonstrate open hostility. Their neutral behaviour may conceal that they have been in contact with the local police or military forces. Unless briefed to the contrary, the survivor/evader should avoid all contact with such people.

Planning and forethought will ensure that a soldier, having made his escape, remains on the run and successfully evades his pursuers.

TRADING WITH LOCALS

In a simple society, where barter trading is common, the soldier can discreetly use salt, tobacco, silver money and similar items when trading with local people. Hard coin is usually good, whether for its exchange value or as jewellery or trinkets. In isolated areas, matches, tobacco, razor blades, empty containers or cloth may be worth more than any form of money. Paper money is always a good bribe, especially if the currency is US dollars. However, the soldier should avoid overpaying; it may lead to embarrassment and even danger. He must always treat people with respect and never bully or ridicule them.

ESCAPE AND EVASION – SIERRA LEONE 2000

A dramatic recent episode of escape and evasion in the British Army occurred in 2000 in the African country of Sierra Leone. In April 2000, at the town of Makeni in north-east Sierra Leone, some 2000 Revolutionary United Front (RUF) fighters were in contact with four United Nations Military Observer (UNMOs) officers – Major Philip Ashby (Royal Marines), Major Andrew Samsonoff (Light Infantry), Major David Lingard of the New Zealand Army and Lieutenant Commander Paul Rowland (Royal Navy).

The officers had enjoyed a reasonable relationship with the RUF until some fighters voluntarily disarmed without the permission. Their commanders regarded them as deserters and demanded that the weapons be returned since they were 'stolen'. On 1 May 2000, RUF fighters surrounded a UN-run disarmament camp near Makeni and a firefight ensued.

Ashby, who had been in the area longer than the other officers, explained that 'Some of the information we were getting from local civilians was that hostility was directed mainly at us, first of all for being British and secondly for being involved in the disarmament process'. The four UNMOs took shelter in a walled compound defended by 70 lightly armed Kenyan UN soldiers. The Kenyans endured several night attacks with small arms and RPGs, and the group decided they should break out and escape to save the Kenyans from further attacks.

Prior to the breakout, Samsonoff contacted his commanding officer, Lt Colonel David Wood MC, by satellite phone. The colonel gave advice that might seem obvious, but which the Light Infantry officer saw as the key to the operation.

'Remember: this is real. It's not an exercise.' As Samsonoff commented later after the initial tension of the escape, it can be easy to switch off during an evasion.

With their faces blackened with charcoal, the four men scaled the wall of the compound at 03.00 hours to leave the town during the night-time RUF curfew. Their escape kit consisted of water, simple rations, map, compass, GPS and first-aid kit. They reasoned that the saving in weight would allow them to move faster.

Fortunately, before relations with the RUF had deteriorated, Ashby had visited the town regularly on his morning runs, so he knew routes past the RUF positions.

They planned to move through the jungle by night and lay up in thickets by day to avoid discovery. Before setting out on their journey, Ashby had contacted his wife, Anna, in the UK by satellite phone. She alerted British officials that the group were on their way.

The plan was to remain in contact with military officials during the trek, but the phone's batteries died after 24 hours.

The group reached a friendly village and a teenage guide was provided to take them to a more secure area. The guide was showing malaria symptoms and had an open stomach wound. Despite this and his flip-flop footwear, he moved rapidly through the jungle and scouted out villages.

Here, while he chatted and shared a cigarette with the locals, the group topped up their water bottles. Since they were now moving by day, they made good time. When they parted with the youthful guide, they gave him money for

Above: Major Phil Ashby (Royal Marines) and Major Andrew Samsonoff relax in Freetown, Sierra Leone, in May 2000, following their successful escape from the Revolutionary United Front.

surgery for his wound and a thanks payment for his village.

'We did at one stage come to a friendly village, where we bought every radio battery in the village, and with the help of our naval officer, who is a qualified nuclear engineer, we attempted to improvise a battery – but sadly it didn't work,' Ashby recalled later. Lt Commander Rowland had wired the batteries in series and in fact the brief signal had been picked up by the British electronic monitoring team in Sierra Leone.

On 12 May, they arrived at the outpost Mile 91, held by Guinean UN troops, and here Philip

Ashby phoned his wife to tell her the group was safe. She in turn was able to pass the information on to the HQ in Freetown and the group was picked up by helicopter. Ashby later said, 'Our main problem was lack of water. It's still the dry season here and although there were rivers marked on our maps, in practice they were in fact pools of stagnant water. We've been drinking some unusually coloured water, shall we say. Our feet are all quite sore and we've got a plethora of exotic insect bites and we're all suffering from prickly heat and a bit of sunburn, but apart from that we're all fine.'

CHAPTER 5

Hiding and Evading

Long-term evaders may need to travel for weeks or even months before reaching friendly territory. However, most Escape and Evasion (E&E) is short-term, lasting anything from about one hour up to 48 hours – typically the time that a pilot is on the ground behind enemy lines.

What is most important in short-term evasion is to understand the few basic anti-capture and anti-tracking techniques. Without this knowledge, the chances are that the evading soldier (or airman, marine etc) will be shot, taken prisoner or recaptured very quickly.

NAVIGATION ON THE RUN

If he is on the run from a PoW camp or holding pen, it is possible that the evader may not have a map or compass. Techniques for locating north using the stars are described in Chapter 2. In daytime, he can find north using the sun and shadows. The earth's relationship to the sun can help him determine direction on earth.

The sun always rises in the east and sets in the west, but not exactly due east or due west. There is also some seasonal variation. In the northern hemisphere, the sun will be due south when at its highest point in the sky, or when an object casts no appreciable shadow. In the southern hemisphere, this same noonday sun will mark due north. In the northern hemisphere, shadows will move clockwise. Shadows will move anti-clockwise in the southern hemisphere. With practice, the evader can use shadows to determine both direction and time of day using the shadow-tip and watch methods.

Left: A Legionnaire of the *3eme Regiment Etranger d'Infanterie* works his way under an obstacle during jungle training in French Guyana. The obstacle course designed by the Legion is particularly testing.

Shadow-Tip Methods

In the first shadow-tip method, the soldier should first find a straight stick 1m (3.2ft) long, and a level spot free of brush on which the stick will cast a definite shadow. This method is simple and accurate and consists of four steps:

Step 1. Place the stick or branch into the ground at a level spot where it will cast a distinctive shadow. Mark the shadow's tip with a stone, twig or other means. This first shadow mark is always west, everywhere on earth.

Step 2. Wait 10–15 minutes until the shadow tip moves a few centimetres and mark the shadow tip's new position in the same way as the first.

Step 3. Draw a straight line through the two marks to obtain an approximate east–west line.

Step 4. Standing with the first mark (west) to the left and the second mark to the right, the soldier is now facing north. This fact is true everywhere on earth.

An alternate method is more accurate, but requires more time. The soldier sets up his shadow stick and marks the first shadow in the morning. He uses a piece of string to draw a clean arc through this mark and around the stick. At midday, the shadow will shrink and disappear. In the afternoon, it will lengthen again and at the point where it touches the arc, he makes a second mark. He draws a line through the two marks to get an accurate east–west line.

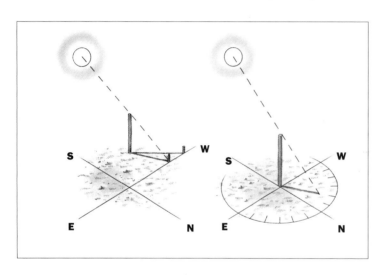

Above: The two shadow tip methods of finding north. The simple, quick method is on the left, the more accurate but slower one on the right. From the perspective of a survivor evading capture, these are useful techniques when he is in a hide and planning to move only at last light.

The Watch Method

The evader can also determine direction using a common, or analogue, watch, a watch with minute and hour hands. The direction will be accurate if he is using true local time, without any changes for daylight savings time. He should remember that the further he is from the equator, the more accurate this method will be. If he has a digital watch, he should quickly draw a watch face on a circle of paper showing the correct time and use it to determine his direction at that time.

In the northern hemisphere, he should hold the watch horizontal and point the hour hand at the sun, then bisect the angle between the hour hand and the 12 o'clock mark to get the north–south line. If there is any doubt as to which end of the line is north, the soldier should remember that the sun rises in the east, sets in the west and is due south at noon. The sun is in the east before noon and in the west after noon. If his watch is set on daylight savings time, he should use the midway point between the hour hand and 1 o'clock to determine the north–south line.

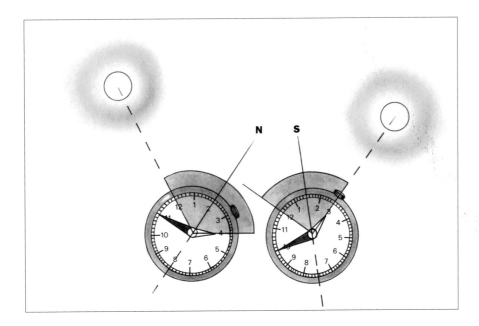

N   S

Left: The watch method
of finding north or south
in the northern and
southern hemispheres
has the advantage for
the survivor/evader
that it can be used on
the move.

IMPROVISED COMPASS

An improvised compass can be constructed using a needle-shaped piece of ferrous metal, or a flat double-edged razor blade, and a piece of non-metallic string or long hair from which to suspend it. The soldier can magnetize or polarize the metal by slowly stroking it in one direction on a piece of silk. or carefully through his hair. using deliberate strokes. He can also polarize metal by stroking it repeatedly at one end with a magnet, remembering always to rub in one direction only. If he has a battery and some electric wire, he can polarize the metal electrically. The wire should be insulated. If not insulated, he can wrap the metal object in a single, thin strip of paper to prevent contact. The battery must be a minimum of two volts. He should form a coil with the electric wire and touch its ends to the battery's terminals. By repeatedly inserting one end of the metal object in and out of the coil, the needle will become an electromagnet. When suspended from a piece of non-metallic string, or floated on a small piece of wood in water, it will align itself with a north–south line.

A more elaborate improvised compass can be constructed using a sewing needle or thin metallic object, a non-metallic container and the silver tip from a pen. To construct this compass, the soldier takes an ordinary sewing needle and breaks it in half. One half will form his direction pointer and the other will act as the pivot point. He should push the portion used as the pivot point through the bottom centre of his container. He attaches one end of the other portion of the needle (the pointer) to the pen's silver tip using glue, tree sap or melted plastic. Finally, he magnetizes the other end of the pointer and rests it on the pivot point.

Above: A US Army special forces soldier pauses to build up his strength during training at Hunter Army Base near Savannah, Georgia. Survival can be taxing for both the body and the spirit, and the encouragement and support found within a small group is vital.

Reading natural signs can also help with survival navigation. Moss growth is lusher on the side of the tree facing the south in the northern hemisphere and vice versa in the southern hemisphere. However, this navigation method is rarely accurate because moss grows completely around some trees. If there are several felled trees around for comparison, look at the stumps. Growth is more vigorous on the side toward the equator and the tree growth rings will be more widely spaced. On the other hand, the tree growth rings will be closer together on the side toward the poles.

Wind direction may be helpful in some instances where there are known prevailing directions.

Recognizing the differences between vegetation and moisture patterns on north- and south-facing slopes can aid in determining direction. In the northern hemisphere, north-facing slopes receive less sun than south-facing slopes and are therefore cooler and damper. In the summer, north-facing slopes at high altitudes may retain patches of snow. In the winter, the trees and open areas on south-facing slopes are the first to lose their snow, and ground-packed snow is shallower.

REST POINTS

Sooner or later, the evader will need to lay-up or rest. He should leave no traces of his presence. He should not assume the 'Hay Barn' mentality. In other words, he should never hide in obvious places. The barn on the hill will look like a tempting refuge in which to hide, but this is also the first place the hunter force will search.

It is a good idea to rest for 5–10 minutes in every hour of travel. The soldier should not just stop anywhere, though. He should choose an area of good cover and try to leave no trace of his LUP (Laying Up Point). When sleeping, he should lie facing the ground, and if he has a ground sheet or something similar, cover himself with it. This should concentrate his scent in one place. If the soldier does not have a sleeping bag, he can use a 'body hollow'. These are body-sized holes, dug about 1–1.3m (3–4ft) deep, and about a foot longer and wider than his body. The hollow is lined with as much soft grass, moss and leaves that he can find. Then, once inside the hollow, he pulls more material onto his body to provide even more insulation. There are numerous variations on the body hollow, such as digging the hollows outward from a central fire pit so heat from the coals keeps him warm at night.

Before he leaves the LUP or stop point, the soldier should 'sterilize' the site – cover his sleeping area with soil and natural debris to mask his scent. He should always bury any food waste, campfire debris, faeces, urine or anything connected with his stay. Waste on the surface will attract flies in warm weather and will be easily spotted by human trackers, and a dog's nose will pick up the scent a long way off. He should try not to contaminate his skin with waste material. Finally, he should cover disturbed soil with natural debris.

Below: Touch is a crucial sense when moving at night. Here a soldier has encountered vegetation that may crunch and be noisy as he moves across it. He will work out a technique to cross this obstacle.

HIDE SITE

After moving for several days, the survivor/evader will move into the area in which he wants to hide and select a hide site. He should keep the following formula in mind when selecting a hide site: BLISS.

B – Blends in with the surroundings.
L – Low in silhouette.
I – Irregular in shape.
S – Small in size.
S – Secluded.

Usually, the soldier's best option will be to crawl into the thickest vegetation he can find. He constructs shelter within the hide area only when essential, such as in cold weather, extreme wet and desert environments. If he builds a shelter, the BLISS formula is his guideline.

When a constructed shelter is a high priority, the soldier's hide area must contain enough material to make the type of shelter he needs, i.e. one that is large enough for him to lie down and sit comfortably. However, he must also remember his tactical situation and the need for safety. He should consider whether the site –

• Provides concealment from enemy observation.
• Has camouflaged escape routes.
• Is suitable for signalling, if necessary.
• Provides protection against wild animals and rocks and dead trees that might fall.
• Is free from insects, reptiles and poisonous plants.

He must also remember the problems that could arise in his environment. For instance, he should avoid building shelters in –
• flash flood areas in foothills.
• avalanche or rockslide areas in mountainous terrain.
• sites near bodies of water that are below the high water mark.

Below: Leaves taken from the local vegetation break up the outline of the jungle hat worn by this soldier, who waits with his face camouflaged and Browning 9mm pistol at the ready.

In some areas, the season of the year has a strong bearing on the site he selects. Ideal sites for a shelter differ in winter and summer. During cold winter months, he will want a site that will protect him from the cold and wind, but which will have a source of fuel and water nearby. During summer months in the same area, he will want a source of water, but he will want the site to be almost insect free.

After the soldier has determined his hide site, he should not move straight into it. He should bypass it and double back in a 'button hook' approach or other deceptive technique, to move to a position outside of the hide site. There he conducts a listening halt before moving into the hide site, being careful not to disturb or cut any vegetation. Once he has occupied the hide site, he should limit his activities to maintaining security, resting, camouflaging and planning his next moves.

If the hide site is occupied by a team, a security rota should be set up. Upon detection of the enemy, the security personnel alert all other personnel, even if the team's plan is to stay hidden and not move upon sighting the enemy. They take this action so that everyone is aware of the danger and ready to react. If any team member leaves the team, he should be given a five-point contingency plan in case the rest of the team have to evacuate the hide site quickly

Camouflage is a very important aspect of both moving and securing a hide site. If there are several hides, team members must check out each other's hides for camouflage and should be honest in their criticisms. When applying natural or man-made materials to the hide, the soldier should not cut vegetation in the immediate area.

Below: Simple field craft techniques for concealment rely on rocks or tree trunks for hiding. Climbing a tree can be good since people are disinclined to look up, but a survivor/evader can become trapped.

Above: A British Royal
Marine from 40
Commando prepares a
shelter in Brunei by
lashing together a
simple frame from which
palm thatching can be
hung to produce a
weatherproof roof.

SHELTER CONSTRUCTION

There are a large variety of shelters which, if circumstances allow, can be constructed to form hide sites and shelters for the soldier on evasion manoeuvres. Poncho Lean-To or Basha shelters take only a short time and minimal equipment to build. The soldier needs his poncho, 2–3m (6.5–10ft) of rope or parachute suspension line, elasticated 'bungees', three stakes about 30cm (12in) long, and two trees or two poles set 2–3m (6.5–10ft) apart. Before selecting the trees or location of the poles, he will check the wind direction, ensuring that the back of his lean-to will be into the wind.

Instructions for making the Poncho Lean-To:

1) Tie off the hood of the poncho, pull the drawstring tight, roll the hood longways, fold it into thirds and tie it off with the drawstring.
2) Cut the rope in half. On one long side of the poncho, tie half of the rope to the corner grommet, then tie the other half to the other corner grommet.
3) Attach a drip stick (a stick about 10cm/4in long) to each rope about 2.5cm

(1in) from the grommet. These drip sticks will keep rainwater from running down the ropes into the lean-to.

4) Tie the ropes about waist high on the trees (uprights). Use a round turn and two half hitches with a quick-release knot.

5) Spread the poncho and anchor it, putting sharpened sticks through the grommets and into the ground.

6) If he plans to use the lean-to for more than one night, or expects rain, he makes a centre support using a line, attaching one end of the line to the poncho hood and the other end to an overhanging branch. He should make sure there is no slack in the line. Another method is to place a stick upright under the centre of the lean-to. This method, however, will restrict his space and movements in the shelter.

For additional protection from wind and rain, some brush, a rucksack, or other equipment can be piled up at the sides of the lean-to. To reduce heat loss to the ground, the floor of the shelter can be lined with some type of insulating material, such as leaves or pine needles. This is important – when at rest, a person could lose as much as 80 percent of his body heat to the ground if sleeping on exposed earth.

To increase security from enemy observation, the soldier lowers the lean-to silhouette by making two changes. First, he secures the support lines to the trees at knee height (not at waist height) using two knee-high sticks in the two centre grommets (sides of lean-to). Second, he angles the poncho to the ground, securing it with sharpened sticks, as above.

Left: Where a poncho or waterproof sheet is available, a shelter can be constructed very quickly by using parachute cord or bungees attached to trees and saplings for support. The sheet can be angled to allow rain to flow off.

The Poncho Tent also provides a low silhouette and protects from the elements on two sides. It has, however, less usable space and observation area than a lean-to. To make this tent, the soldier needs a poncho, two 1.5–2.5m (5–8ft) ropes, six sharpened sticks about 30cm (12in) long and two trees 2–3m (6.5–10ft) apart.

Instructions for making a Poncho Tent:

1) Tie off the poncho hood in the same way as the Poncho Lean-To.
2) Tie a 2–3m (6.5–10ft) rope to the centre grommet on each side of the poncho.
3) Tie the other ends of these ropes at about knee height to two trees 2–3m (6.5–10ft) and stretch the poncho tight.
4) Draw one side of the poncho tight and secure it to the ground, pushing sharpened sticks through the grommets. Follow the same procedure on the other side.

If he needs a centre support, he should use the same methods as for the Poncho Lean-To. Another centre support is an A-frame set outside and over the centre of the tent, using two 90–120cm (35–47in) long sticks, one with a forked end, to form the A-frame. The poncho hood's draw-string is tied to the A-frame to support the centre of the tent.

If the survivor/evader is a pilot and has a parachute and three poles, and if the tactical situation allows, he can make a Parachute Tepee. It is easy and takes very little time to make this tepee. It provides protection from the elements and can act as a signalling device by enhancing a small amount of light from a fire or candle to form a luminous shelter. It is large enough to hold several people and their equipment and to allow sleeping, cooking and storing firewood.

He can make this tepee using parts of or a whole personnel main or reserve parachute canopy. If using a standard personnel parachute, he needs three poles 3.5–4.5m (11–15ft) long and about 5cm (2in) in diameter.

Instructions for a Parachute Tepee:

1) Lay the poles on the ground and lash them together at one end.
2) Stand the framework up and spread the poles to form a tripod.
3) For more support, place additional poles against the tripod. Five or six additional poles work best, but do not lash them to the tripod.
4) Determine the wind direction and locate the entrance 90° or more from the mean wind direction.
5) Lay out the parachute on the 'backside' of the tripod and locate the bridle loop (nylon web loop) at the top (apex) of the canopy.
6) Place the bridle loop over the top of a free-standing pole. Then place the pole back up against the tripod so that the canopy's apex is at the same height as the lashing on the three poles.

7) Wrap the canopy around one side of the tripod. The canopy should be of double thickness, as an entire parachute being used. Only half of the tripod need be wrapped, as the remainder of the canopy will encircle the tripod in the opposite direction.

8) Construct the entrance by wrapping the folded edges of the canopy around two free-standing poles. The poles can then be placed side by side to close the tepee's entrance.

9) All extra canopy is placed underneath the tepee poles and inside to create a floor for the shelter.

Above: With a simple frame to support the leaves that have been positioned to overlap like a slate roof, a soldier and his kit can stay protected even from tropical rain.

It is essential to leave a 30–50cm (12–20in) opening at the top for ventilation if intending to have a fire inside the tepee.

A variation on the Parachute Tepee is the One-Pole Parachute Tepee. For this, the survivor needs a 14-gore section (normally) of canopy, stakes, a stout centre pole, and inner core and needle. He cuts the suspension lines, except for 40–45cm (16–18in) lengths at the canopy's lower lateral band.

Instructions for the One-Pole Parachute Tepee:

1) Select a shelter site and scribe a circle about 4m (13ft) in diameter on the ground.

2) Stake the parachute material to the ground using the lines remaining at the lower lateral band.

3) After deciding where to place the shelter door, emplace a stake and tie the first line (from the lower lateral band) securely to it.

4) Stretch the parachute material taut to the next line, emplace a stake on the scribed line, and tie the line to it.

5) Continue the staking process until all the lines are tied.

6) Loosely attach the top of the parachute material to the centre pole with a suspension line previously cut and, through trial and error, determine the point at which the parachute material will be pulled tight once the centre pole is upright. Then securely attach the material to the pole.

7) Using a suspension line (or inner core), sew the end gores together leaving 1m (3ft) gap for a door.

Below: A British RAF aircrew uses a parachute draped over a basic frame for protection. He has lit a fire to provide warmth and to cook food. His kindling and a wood store are with him under the shelter.

To construct the No-Pole Parachute Tepee, the survivor/evader uses the same materials, except for the centre pole, as for the one-pole parachute tepee.

Instructions for making the No-Pole Parachute Tepee:

1) Tie a line to the top of parachute material with a previously cut suspension line. Throw the line over a tree limb, and tie it to the tree trunk.

2) Starting at the opposite side from the door, emplace a stake on a scribed 3.5–4m (11–13ft) circle.

3) Tie the first line on the lower lateral band and continue emplacing the stakes and tying the lines to them.

4) After staking down the material, unfasten the line tied to the tree trunk, tighten the tepee material by pulling on this line and tie it securely to the tree trunk.

For warmth and ease of construction, the Debris Hut is one of the best shelters.

FIELD-EXPEDIENT LEAN-TO

If the survivor/evader is in a wooded area and has enough natural materials, he can make a Field-Expedient Lean-to without the aid of tools or with only a knife. It takes longer to make this type of shelter than it does to make other types, but it will protect him from the elements.

He will need two trees (or upright poles) about 2m (6.5ft) apart; one pole about 2m (6.5ft) long and 2.5cm (1in) in diameter; five to eight poles about 3m (10ft) long and 2.5cm (1in) in diameter for beams; cord or vines for securing the horizontal support to the trees; and other poles, saplings or vines to criss-cross the beams.

Above: The field-expedient lean-to takes time, and within a group it would make sense for other members to be gathering food and water while it is being prepared since the onset of darkness will make all these operations impossible.

INSTRUCTIONS FOR MAKING THE FIELD-EXPEDIENT LEAN-TO:

1) Tie the 2m (6.5ft) pole to the two trees at waist to chest height. This is the horizontal support. If a standing tree is not available, construct a bipod using Y-shaped sticks or two tripods.

2) Place one end of the beams (3m/10ft poles) on one side of the horizontal support.

3) Criss-cross saplings or vines on the beams.

4) Cover the framework with brush, leaves, pine needles or grass, starting at the bottom and working up like shingling.

5) Place straw, leaves, pine needles or grass inside the shelter for bedding.

In cold weather, the soldier can add to his lean-to's comfort by building a fire reflector wall. He drives four 1.5m (5ft) stakes into the ground to support the wall and then stacks green logs on top of one another between the support stakes, forming two rows of stacked logs to create an inner space within the wall that he can fill with dirt. This action not only strengthens the wall but makes it more heat-reflective. He binds the top of the support stakes so that the green logs and dirt will stay in place.

Instructions for making a debris hut:

1) Make a tripod with two short stakes and a long ridgepole (running the length of the shelter) or by placing one end of a long ridgepole on top of a sturdy base.

2) Secure the ridgepole using the tripod method or by anchoring it to a tree at about waist height.

3) Prop large sticks along both sides of the ridgepole to create a wedge-shaped ribbing effect. Ensure the ribbing is wide enough to accommodate the body and steep enough to shed moisture.

4) Place finer sticks and brush crosswise on the ribbing. These form a latticework that will keep the insulating material (grass, pine needles, leaves) from falling through the ribbing into the sleeping area.

5) Add light, dry (if possible), soft debris over the ribbing until the insulating material is at least 1m (3ft) thick – the thicker, the better.

6) Place a 30cm (12in) layer of insulating material inside the shelter. At the entrance, pile insulating material for closing the improvising a door.

7) As a final step in constructing this shelter, add shingling material or branches on top of the debris layer to prevent the insulating material from blowing away in a storm.

NATURAL SHELTERS

A soldier on evasion may not have the time or opportunity to construct a shelter, so he should not overlook natural formations that provide shelter. Examples include caves, rocky crevices, clumps of bushes, small depressions, large rocks on the leeward sides of hills, large trees with low-hanging limbs, and fallen trees with thick branches. When selecting a natural shelter, however, he needs to be aware of the following:

• He should stay away from low ground such as ravines, narrow valleys or creek beds. Low areas collect the heavy cold air at night and are therefore colder than

TREE-PIT SHELTER

If the evader is in a cold, snow-covered area where evergreen trees grow and he has a digging tool, he can make a Tree-Pit Shelter.

1) Find a tree with bushy branches that provide overhead cover.

2) Dig out the snow around the tree trunk until the desired depth and diameter is reached, or until the ground is exposed.

3) Pack the snow around the top and the inside of the hole to provide support.

4) Find and cut other evergreen boughs. Place them over the top of the pit to give overhead cover. Place other boughs in the bottom of the pit for insulation.

the surrounding high ground. Thick, brushy, low ground also harbours more insects.

- He should check for poisonous snakes, ticks, mites, scorpions and stinging ants.
- He must look for loose rocks, dead branches, coconuts or other natural growth that could fall on his shelter.

In an arid environment like a desert, the survivor/evader who has material such as a poncho, canvas or a parachute, can use it along with such terrain features as rock outcropping, mounds of sand or a depression between dunes or rocks to make his shelter. Using rock outcroppings, he anchors one end of his poncho (or other material) on the edge of the outcrop with rocks or other weights, then extends and anchors the other end of the poncho so it provides the best possible shade. In a sandy area, he can build a mound of sand or use the side of a sand dune for one side of the shelter. If he has enough material, he can fold it in half and form a

Left: In the jungle, it is advisable to build a platform to stay above the ground in order to avoid pests and snakes. If mosquitoes are a problem, a small smoky fire will help to keep them away, but may reveal the hide.

BEACH SHADE SHELTER

At the warmer end of the climatic spectrum, the Beach Shade Shelter protects the soldier from the sun, wind, rain and heat. It is easy to make using natural materials. To make a Beach Shade Shelter:

1) Find and collect driftwood or other natural material to use as support beams and as digging tools.

2) Select a site above the high-water mark.

3) Scrape or dig out a trench running north to south so that it receives the least amount of sunlight. Make the trench long and wide enough to lie down comfortably.

4) Mound soil or sand on three sides of the trench. The higher the mound, the more space inside the shelter.

5) Lay support beams (driftwood or other natural material) that span the trench on top of the mound, to form the framework for a roof.

6) Enlarge the shelter's entrance by digging out more sand in front of it.

7) Use natural materials, such as grass or leaves, to form a bed inside the shelter.

30–45cm (12–18in) airspace between the two halves. This layering of the material will reduce the inside temperature to between 11°C and 22°C (20–40°F).

A subterranean shelter will have a similar heat-reducing effect. Building it, however, requires more time and effort than for other shelters. Since his physical effort will make the soldier sweat more and increase dehydration, he must construct it before the heat of the day.

To make a subterranean shelter, he finds a low spot or depression between dunes or rocks, or digs a trench 45–60cm (18–24in) deep and long and wide enough for him to lie in comfortably. Next he piles the sand he takes from the trench to form a mound around three sides.

On the open end of the trench, he then digs out more sand so he can get in and out of his shelter easily, before covering the trench with his material. Finally he secures the material in place using sand, rocks or other weights.

HIDE OPERATING PROCEDURES

Once the hide is built and secure, the soldier can plan his next actions. All team members are informed of both their current location and an alternate hide site location designated for emergencies. Once this is done, planning begins for the team's next movement.

Planning the team's movement begins with a map reconnaissance. The next hide area is selected first, then a primary and an alternate route to the existing hide area. In choosing the routes, straight lines are avoided and they should involve one or two radical changes in direction. Routes which offer the best cover and concealment, the fewest obstacles and the least likelihood of contact with humans are preferred. There should be locations along the route where the team can get water. To aid team navigation, azimuths, distances, checkpoints or steering marks and corridors are used, and rally points and rendezvous points are set at intervals along the route.

Once evasion and security planning is complete, everyone should memorize the entire plan. The team members should know the distances and bearings for the entire route to the next hide area. They should study the map and know the various terrain they will be moving across so that they can move without using the map.

A trained team will not occupy a hide site for more than 24 hours. In most situations, they hide during the day and move at night. Actions are strictly limited while in a hide. Movement should be restricted to less than 45cm (18in) above the ground, and no fires or food cooking is usually allowed – smoke and food odours will reveal the hide location. Before leaving the hide site, the team will sterilize it (remove signs of the team's presence) to prevent tracking.

Building a hide or shelter is an essential evasion skill to prevent enemy detection. However, the environment may actually be a bigger danger than the enemy in many terrains, so we will now look at the essential survival skills a soldier must take with him into the field

Below: In thick vegetation, a young US Marine glances back to check whether he is being followed. Maintaining silence is essential if an escaper/evader is to avoid being detected.

CHAPTER 6

Evasion and Survival

Escape and evasion is as much about surviving the natural elements as avoiding the enemy. Without sound basic survival skills, the soldier on the run may be in more danger from the climate and terrain than enemy soldiers.

One important aspect of prior survival planning is preventive medicine. The soldier should ensure that he has no dental problems and that his immunizations are current – these will help the survivor/evader avoid troublesome dental or health issues in the field. A dental problem in a survival situation will reduce his ability to cope with other difficulties that he faces. Failure to keep his shots current may mean his body is not immune to diseases that are prevalent in the area.

SURVIVAL KIT

Preparing and carrying a survival kit is as important as the health considerations mentioned above. All US military aircraft normally have survival kits on board for the type of areas over which they will fly. There are kits for over-water survival, for hot climate survival and an aviator survival vest. There is also an individual survival kit with general packet and medical packet. The cold climate, hot climate and over-water kits are in canvas carrying bags. These kits are normally stowed in the helicopter's cargo/passenger area. An aviator's survival vest (SRU-21P), worn by helicopter crews, also contains survival items. US Army aviators flying fixed-wing aircraft equipped with ejection seats use the SRFU-31/P survival vest. The

Left: A French Foreign Legion paratrooper crosses a water obstacle at the French Army's Commando Training School at Mont Louis in the Pyrenees. Testing exercises allow soldiers to learn their limits and discover that they can go beyond them.

individual survival kits are stowed in the seat pan. Like all other kits, the particular rigid seat survival kit (RSSK) depends on the environment. If he is not an aviator, he will probably not have access to the survival vests or survival kits. However, if he knows what these kits contain, it will help him to plan and to prepare his own survival kit. Even the smallest survival kit, if properly prepared, is invaluable when faced with a survival problem. Before making his survival kit, however, the soldier should consider the unit mission, the operational environment and the equipment and vehicles assigned to his unit.

Right: A US Apache helicopter pilot shows the 2003 survival kit. It includes an oxygen cylinder that gives 10 minutes of air supply under water, an inflatable life raft, a GPS device, handgun, distress marker and emergency rations.

The environment is the key to the types of items he will need in his survival kit. How much equipment he puts in his kit depends on how he will carry the kit. A kit carried on his body will have to be smaller than one carried in a vehicle. He should always layer his survival kit, keeping the most important items on his body. For example, his map and compass should always be in his clothing. He should carry less important items on his load-bearing equipment and place bulky items in the rucksack.

In preparing his survival kit, he selects items he can use for more than one purpose. Generally speaking, items should not be duplicated, as this increases the kit's size and weight.

His survival kit need not be elaborate. He needs only functional items that will meet his needs and a case to hold the items. For the case, he might want to use a tobacco tin, the tough plastic US Army first aid or decontamination case, or an ammunition pouch. The case should be water-repellent or waterproof; easy to carry or attach to his body; suitable to accept different-sized components; and durable.

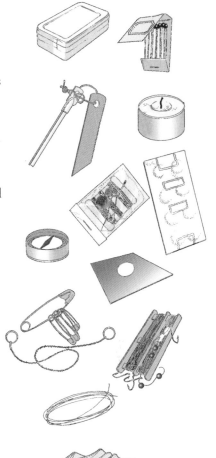

In his survival kit, he should have:
- Water purification tablets.
- Fire-starting equipment.
- Food procurement items.
- First aid items.
- Signalling items.
- Shelter items.

Some examples of these items are:
- Lighter, metal match, waterproof matches.
- Signalling mirror.
- Fish and snare line.
- Candle.
- Oxytetracycline tablets
(for treating diarrhoea or infection).
- Water purification tablets.
- Surgical blades.
- Condoms for water storage.
- A weapon (only if the situation so dictates).
- Snare wire.
- Wrist compass.
- Fishhooks.
- Small hand lens.
- Needle and thread.
- Knife.
- Solar blanket.
- Butterfly sutures.
- Chap Stick.

He should read about and practice the survival techniques skills like fishing and hunting. However good the equipment that an evader may be carrying in a survival environment, if he has not used it and become confident in training he will find it very difficult to learn on the job.

He should first consider his unit's mission and the environment in which his unit will operate, then prepare his survival kit.

Above: Items found in a survival tin (top) include matches, flint and steel, candle, pain killers, sewing kit, compass, signal mirror, safety pins, snare/wire saw, fishing kit and line, water filtration bag and water purifying tablets.

FINDING WATER

The human body loses water through normal body processes (sweating, urinating and defecating). During average daily exertion when the atmospheric temperature is 20° C (68°F), the average adult loses and therefore requires 2–3 litres (3.5–5 pints) of water daily. Other factors, such as heat exposure, cold exposure, intense activity, high altitude, burns or illness can cause the body to lose more water. This water must be replaced.

Dehydration results from inadequate replacement of lost body fluids. It decreases efficiency and, if the survivor/evader is injured, increases his susceptibility to severe shock. Consider the following results of body fluid loss:

- A 5 per cent loss of body fluids results in thirst, irritability, nausea and weakness.
- A 10 per cent loss results in dizziness, headache, inability to walk and a tingling sensation in the limbs.
- A 15 per cent loss results in dim vision, painful urination, swollen tongue, deafness and a numb feeling in the skin.
- A loss greater than 15 per cent of body fluids may result in death.

The most common signs and symptoms of dehydration are:

- Dark urine with a very strong odour.
- Dark, sunken eyes.
- Emotional instability.
- Delayed capillary refill in fingernail beds.
- Low urine output.
- Fatigue.
- Loss of skin elasticity.
- Trench line down centre of tongue.

Opposite: A British Royal Marine of 40 Commando constructs a water catcher while on a jungle training exercise in Brunei. The stick tripod and leaves are a natural bowl that will collect clean rainwater – important where water sources may be polluted.

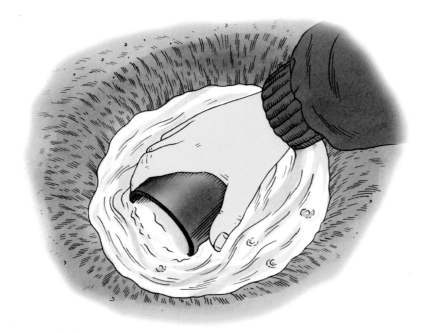

Left: If a stream is murky, one option is to dig a hole a short distance from the bank and let the ground act as a filter to produce clear water – it will, however, still need to be sterilized.

• Thirst. This is last on the list because the survivor/evader is already 2 per cent dehydrated by the time he starts to crave fluids.

He must replace the water as he loses it. Trying to make up a deficit is difficult in a survival situation and, as mentioned earlier, thirst is not a sign of how much water he needs.

Most people cannot comfortably drink more than 1 litre (1.7 pints) of water at a time. So, even when not thirsty, the evader should drink small amounts of water at regular intervals each hour to prevent dehydration. If he is under physical and mental stress or subject to severe conditions, he should increase his water intake, drinking enough liquids to maintain a urine output of at least 500ml (0.8 pints) every 24 hours.

In any situation where food intake is low, he should drink 6–8 litres (10–14 pints) of water per day. In an extreme climate, especially an arid one, the average

Right: A jungle waterfall is not only a source of potential drinking water, but also a natural shower bath. The survivor/evader will have the chance to clean off mud and sweat and reduce the risk of jungle skin infections.

ESTIMATING FLUID LOSS

A soldier on the run can estimate fluid loss by several means. A standard field dressing soaks up about a 250ml (0.4 pints) of blood. A soaked T-shirt holds 500-750ml (1.3 pints). He can also use the pulse and breathing rate to estimate fluid loss, using the following as a guide:

1) With 750ml (1.3 pints) loss, the wrist pulse rate will be under 100 beats per minute and the breathing rate 12 to 20 breaths per minute.

2) With 0.75–1.5 litres (1.3–2.6 pints), loss the pulse rate will be 100 to 120 beats per minute and 20 to 30 breaths per minute.

3) With a 1.5–2 litres (2.6–3.5 pints) loss, the pulse rate will be 120 to 140 beats per minute and 30 to 40 breaths per minute. Vital signs above these rates signal a requirement for more advanced care than simple rehydration. This may include treatments used for acute diahorea or even the administration of a saline drip.

person can lose 2.5–3.5 litres (4–6 pints) of water per hour. In this type of climate, he should drink 14–30 litres (25–53 pints) of water per day. With the loss of water, there is also a loss of electrolytes (body salts). The average diet can usually keep up with these losses, but in an extreme situation or illness, additional sources need to be provided. A mixture of a quarter of a teaspoon of salt to 1 litre (1.7 pints) of water will provide a concentration that the body tissues can readily absorb.

Of all the physical problems encountered in a survival situation, the loss of water is the most preventable. The following are basic guidelines for the prevention of dehydration:

• Always drink water when eating. Water is used and consumed as a part of the digestion process, and not drinking while eating can lead to dehydration.

• Acclimatize. The body performs more efficiently in extreme conditions when acclimatized to environment.

• Conserve sweat not water. Limit sweat-producing activities, but drink water.

• Ration water. Until the soldier finds a suitable source, he should use water sensibly. A daily intake of 500ml (0.8 pints) of a sugar-water mixture (two teaspoons per litre) will suffice to prevent severe dehydration for at least a week, but only if he keeps water losses to a minimum by strictly limiting activity and exposure to heat.

Water can be collected from several natural sources. Rainwater collected in clean containers or in plants is usually safe for drinking. However, the soldier should purify water from lakes, ponds, swamps, springs or streams, especially the water near human settlements or in the tropics. He must purify all water taken from

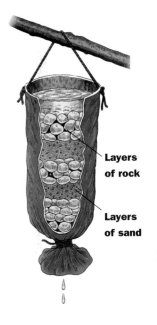

Layers
of rock

Layers
of sand

Above: Water filters should consist of multiple layers of filtering material to remove the full range of particles suspended in the water.

vegetation or from the ground by using iodine or chlorine, or by boiling. Water is purified by:

- Using water purification tablets (following the directions provided).
- Placing five drops of 2 percent tincture of iodine in a canteen full of clear water. If the canteen is full of cloudy or cold water, 10 drops are used and a canteen of water should stand for 30 minutes before drinking.
- Boiling water for one minute at sea level, adding one minute for each additional 300m (984ft) above sea level, or boil for 10 minutes no matter where the survivor/evader is.

SOLAR STILL

One invaluable survival aid that the survivor can use for collecting water is the solar still. The British Airborne Industries still is an inflatable unit that can produce drinking water from seawater or impure water sources. It is primarily intended for use in emergency situations and is widely used as an integral part of military survival packs. A typical Airborne solar still has an inflated diameter of about 775mm (30in) and a height of 540mm (21in).

The solar still consists of an inflatable buoyancy ring that allows the unit to float on water if required. Inside the ring is a black solar collector with a reservoir for impure water underneath. Above the solar collector is a clear cone. Impure water is fed into the solar collector where it evaporates, the water vapour condensing on the inside of the clear cone. The purified water runs down the inside of the cone into a collecting gutter, from where it runs into an external collecting bag for use.

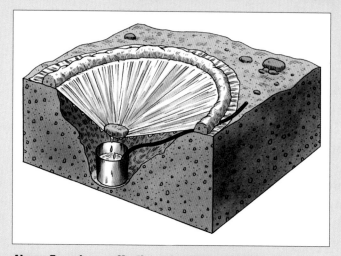

Above: To make an effective solar still, seal the perimeter of plastic sheeting tightly to the ground so that no captured water vapour is allowed to escape.

The performance of the solar still will depend on the level of solar radiation received and this, in turn, is dependent on the geographic location and the local climate. Typical examples are: in the UK on an average February day the still will produce 500ml (0.8 pints); on an average March day in the Indian Ocean it will produce 1.5 litres (2.6 pints); and on an October day in North Africa, 1.685 litres (3 pints) will be produced.

Left: A rudimentary
water collector made
from a leaf stiffened by
a twig and attached to
a tree. This device was
constructed by soldiers
of the 1st Battalion,
The Grenadier Guards
in Brunei.

By drinking non-potable water, the survivor/evader may contract diseases or swallow organisms that can harm him. Examples of such diseases or organisms are:

Dysentery – Severe, prolonged diarrhoea with bloody stools, fever and weakness.
Cholera and typhoid – The soldier may be susceptible to these diseases regardless of inoculations.
Flukes – Stagnant, polluted water, especially in tropical areas, often contains blood flukes. If a person swallows flukes, they will bore into his bloodstream, live as parasites, and cause disease.
Leeches – If a leech is swallowed, it can hook onto the throat passage or inside the nose. It will suck blood, create a wound and move to another area. Each bleeding wound may become infected.

If the water is also muddy, stagnant and foul-smelling, the survivor/evader can clear it by placing it in a container and letting it stand for 12 hours and by pouring it through a filtering system. These procedures, however, only clear the water and make it more palatable. It will still need purification.

A filtering system is made by placing several layers of filtering material, such as sand, crushed rock, charcoal, cloth-filled bamboo or an article of clothing, on top of one another in strata several centimetres thick each. The water is then poured through the filter to clean it. Remove the odour from water by adding charcoal. Let the water stand for 45 minutes before drinking it.

UNIVERSAL EDIBILITY TEST

The Universal Edibility Test is used to establish whether plants are edible when positive identification of the plant type cannot be made. This test requires considerable patience. Always practise the following method:

1) Test only one part of a potential food plant at a time.

2) Separate the plant into its basic components – leaves, stems, roots, buds and flowers.

3) Smell the food for strong acid odours. Remember, smell alone does not indicate that a plant is edible or inedible.

4) Do not eat for eight hours before starting the test.

5) During the eight hours you abstain from eating, test for contact poisoning by placing a piece of the plant part you are testing on the inside of your elbow or wrist. Usually 15 minutes is enough time to allow for a reaction.

6) During the test period, take nothing by mouth except purified water and the plant you are testing.

7) Select a small portion of a single plant and prepare it the way you plan to eat it.

8) Before placing the prepared plant in your mouth, touch a small portion (a pinch) to the outer surface of your lip to test for burning or itching.

9) If, after three minutes, there is no reaction on your lip, place the plant part on your tongue, holding it there for at least 15 minutes.

10) If there is no reaction, thoroughly chew a pinch and hold it in your mouth for 15 minutes. Do not swallow.

11) If no burning, itching, numbing, stinging or other irritation occurs during 15 minutes, swallow the food.

12) Wait eight hours. If any ill effects occur during this period, induce vomiting and drink a lot of water.

13) If no ill effects occur, eat a quarter of a cup of the same plant part prepared exactly the same way. Wait another eight hours. If no ill effects occur, the plant part as prepared is safe for eating.

FOOD

Although a survivor/evader can live several weeks without food, he needs an adequate amount to stay healthy. Without food, his mental and physical capabilities will deteriorate rapidly, and he will become weak. Food replenishes the substances that the body burns and provides energy. It provides vitamins, minerals, salts and other elements essential to good health. Possibly more important, it helps morale.

The two basic sources of food are plants and animals (including fish). In varying degrees, both provide the calories, carbohydrates, fats and proteins needed for normal daily body functions.

Calories are a measure of heat and potential energy. The average person needs 2000 calories per day to function at a minimum level. An adequate balance of carbohydrates, fats and proteins without an adequate calorific intake will lead to starvation and cannibalism of the body's own tissue for energy.

PLANT FOODS

Plant foods provide carbohydrates – the main source of energy. As vegetarian diets show, many plants provide enough protein to keep the body at normal efficiency. Although plants may not provide a balanced diet, they will sustain even in the arctic, where meat's heat-producing qualities are normally essential. Many plant foods such as nuts and seeds will give enough protein and oils for normal efficiency. Roots, green vegetables and plant food containing natural sugar will provide calories and carbohydrates that give the body natural energy.

The food value of plants becomes more and more important if the soldier is eluding the enemy or if he is in an area where wildlife is scarce. He can obtain plants more easily and more quietly than meat. This is extremely important when the enemy is near. He can also dry plants by wind, air, sun or fire. This retards spoilage so that he can store or carry the plant food to use when needed.

False Friends

Poison hemlock has killed people who mistook it for its relatives, wild carrots and wild parsnips. Fungi are best avoided, as they are not very nutritious and even in countries like Russia, France and Italy, where people hunt for wild mushrooms, there are numerous cases of poisoning through misidentification.

At times, the survivor/evader may find himself in a situation for which he could not plan. In this case, he may not have had the chance to learn the plant life of the region in which he must survive. Using the Universal Edibility Test (see feature box) will help him determine which plants he can eat and those to avoid.

It is important for the soldier to be able to recognize both cultivated and wild edible plants in a survival situation. If he picks cultivated plants, he should take

Left: To dig up a root, first sharpen a long, straight stick on one side so that it forms a chisel-like edge. Insert the stick down the side of a plant and chisel away until the root is well exposed. Then use the stick to lever the root to the surface without causing damage to the root.

care that this does not compromise his safety and security. He should remember the following when collecting wild plants for food:

Plants growing near homes and occupied buildings or along roadsides may have been sprayed with pesticides and require thorough washing. In more highly developed countries with many automobiles, roadside plants are, if possible, to be avoided due to contamination from exhaust emissions.

Plants growing in contaminated water or in water containing Giardia lamblia and other parasites are contaminated themselves, and should be boiled or disinfected.

Some plants develop extremely dangerous fungal toxins. To lessen the chance of accidental poisoning, the soldier must not eat any fruit that is starting to spoil or showing signs of mildew or fungus.

Plants of the same species may differ in their toxic or subtoxic compounds content because of genetic or environmental factors. One example of this is the foliage of the common chokecherry. Some chokecherry plants have high concentrations of deadly cyanide compounds while others have low concentrations or none. Horses have died from eating wilted wild cherry leaves. Avoid any weeds, leaves or seeds with an almond-like scent, a characteristic of the cyanide compounds.

Some people are more susceptible to gastric distress from plants than others. If the survivor/evader is sensitive in this way, he should avoid unknown wild plants. If he is extremely sensitive to poison ivy, he should steer clear of plants from this family, including any parts from sumacs, mangoes and cashews.

Some edible wild plants, such as acorns and water lily rhizomes, are bitter. The bitter substances, usually tannin compounds, make them unpalatable. Boiling them in several changes of water will usually remove these bitter properties.

Many valuable wild plants have high concentrations of oxalate compounds, also known as oxalic acid. Oxalates produce a sharp burning sensation in the mouth and throat and damage the kidneys. Baking, roasting or drying usually

Right: Certain plant substances, such as pine needles, are suitable for producing drinks through the infusion method. First, crush the needles with a large stone (A). Then tip the needles into boiling water and allow the mix to sit for up to 10 minutes, stirring occasionally (B). Finally, strain the fluid through a piece of cloth into a vessel (C) and drink.

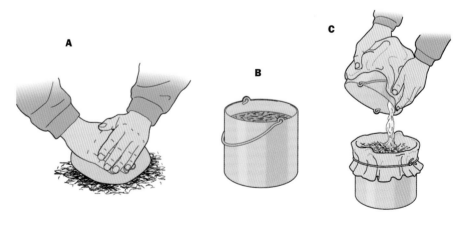

PREPARING PLANT FOODS

Although some plants or plant parts are edible raw, the soldier must cook others to make them edible or palatable – edible to provide him with necessary nutrients and palatable to make it pleasing to eat. Many wild plants are edible but barely palatable.

Methods used to improve the taste of plant food are similar to those used in the kitchen and include soaking, boiling, cooking or leaching. Leaching is done by crushing the food (for example, acorns), placing it in a strainer and pouring boiling water through it or immersing it in running water. Leaves, stems and buds should be boiled until tender, changing the water, if necessary, to remove any bitterness. Tubers and roots can be boiled, baked or roasted. Drying helps to remove caustic oxalates from some roots, like those in the Arum family. Acorns are leached in water to remove the bitterness. Some nuts, such as chestnuts, are good raw, but taste better roasted. The soldier can eat many grains and seeds raw until they mature. When hard or dry, he may have to boil or grind them into meal or flour. Plants are very versatile and the survivor/evader will find other uses for them than just nourishment. He can make dyes from various plants to colour clothing or to camouflage his skin. Usually, he will have to boil the plants to get the best results. Onion skins produce yellow, walnut hulls produce brown and pokeberries provide a purple dye. Fibres and cordage can be made from plant fibres. Most commonly used are the stems from nettles and milkweeds, yucca plants and the inner bark of trees like the linden.

Fish poison is produced by immersing walnut hulls in a small area of quiet water. This poison makes it impossible for the fish to breathe and forces them to the surface; it does not, however, render them inedible.

Tinder for starting fires can be made from cattail fluff, cedar bark, lighter knot wood from pine trees, or hardened sap from resinous wood trees. The soldier can make insulation for a sleeping hole or his clothing by fluffing up female cattail heads or milkweed down. Insect repellents can be produced by applying the juice of wild garlic or onion to the skin, by placing sassafras leaves in a shelter, or by burning or smudging cattail seed hair fibres.

destroys these oxalate crystals. The corm (bulb) of the jack-in-the-pulpit is known as the 'Indian turnip', but the survivor/evader can eat it only after removing these crystals by slow baking or by drying.

ANIMAL FOODS

Meat is more nourishing than plant food. In fact, it may even be more readily available in some places. However, to get meat, the soldier engaged in survival and evasion will need to know the habits of, and how to capture, the various types of wildlife. To satisfy his immediate food needs, he should first seek the more abundant and more easily obtained wildlife, such as insects, crustaceans, molluscs,

Right: British Territorial
Army troopers of 21
Special Air Service
(SAS) cook a rabbit over
a fire during a survival
and evasion exercise in
the Brecon Beacons,
South Wales. It is a
rudimentary spit roast.

Right: British Territorial Army troopers of 21 Special Air Service (SAS) cook a rabbit over a fire during a survival and evasion exercise in the Brecon Beacons, South Wales. It is a rudimentary spit roast.

fish and reptiles. These can satisfy his immediate hunger while he prepares traps and snares for larger game.

Mammals are excellent protein sources and, for Europeans and North Americans, the most tasty food source. There are some drawbacks to obtaining mammals. In a hostile environment, the enemy may detect any traps or snares placed on land. The amount of injury an animal can inflict is in direct proportion to its size. All mammals have teeth and nearly all will bite in self-defence. Even a squirrel can inflict a serious wound and any bite presents a serious risk of infection. Also, a mother can be extremely aggressive in defence of her young. Any animal with no route of escape will fight when cornered.

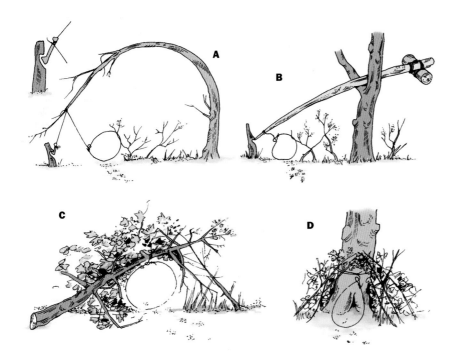

Left: A variety of different snares can be used to catch animals. Snares can use spring tension (A) or counterweight tension (B) to lift the animal off the ground when it is snared. Through careful positioning of vegetation, an animal can be channelled to move into the snare (C and D).

All mammals are edible. However, the Polar Bear and Bearded Seal have toxic levels of vitamin A in their livers. The Platypus, native to Australia and Tasmania, is an egg-laying, semi-aquatic mammal that has poisonous glands. Scavenging mammals, such as the Opossum, may carry diseases

Unless the survivor has the chance to take large game, he should concentrate his efforts on the smaller animals, due to their abundance. The smaller animal species are also easier to prepare. He need not know all the animal species that are suitable as food, since relatively few are poisonous, and they make a smaller list to remember. What is important is to learn the habits and behavioural patterns of different classes of animals – for example, animals that are excellent choices for trapping, those that inhabit a particular range and occupy a den or nest, those that have somewhat fixed feeding areas, and those that have trails leading from one area to another. Larger, herding animals, such as elk or caribou, roam vast areas and are somewhat more difficult to trap.

Insects

The first obstacle to eating insects is overcoming the natural aversion to their appearance. Historically, people in starvation situations have resorted to eating everything imaginable for nourishment. A person who ignores an otherwise healthy food source due to a personal bias, or because he feels it is unappetizing, is risking his own survival. Although it may prove difficult at first, a survivor must eat what is available to maintain his health.

Insects are the most abundant life-form on earth and are easily caught. Insects provide 65–80 per cent protein compared to 20 per cent for beef. This fact makes insects an important, if not overly appetizing, food source. Insects to avoid include all that sting or bite, hairy or brightly coloured insects, and caterpillars and insects that have a pungent odour. Also, spiders and common disease carriers such as ticks, flies and mosquitoes should not be a part of a survival diet.

Right: Two soldiers from the Pathfinder Platoon prepare a deadfall animal trap during an escape and evasion course. The trap would become effective only after being left for several days to allow the human scent to dissipate.

BIRDS AS FOOD

All species of birds are edible, although the flavour will vary considerably. It is advisable to skin fish-eating birds to improve their taste. As with any wild animal, the soldier in the wild must understand birds' common habits to have a realistic chance of capturing them. He can take pigeons, as well as some other species, from their roost at night by hand. During the nesting season, some species will not leave the nest even when approached. Knowing where and when the birds nest makes catching them easier. Birds tend to have regular routes from the roost to a feeding area or water. Careful observation should reveal these routes and indicate good areas for netting birds. Roosting sites and waterholes are some of the most promising areas for trapping or snaring.

Nesting birds present another food source – eggs. The soldier should remove all but two or three eggs from the clutch, marking those that have been left. The bird will continue to lay more eggs to fill the clutch, so the soldier can continue removing the fresh eggs, leaving the marked ones.

Birds can also be trapped by digging a trench sloping down to about 20cm (8in) deep in an area where dove and quail have been seen. The trench should be about 60cm (2ft) long. Over the deep end of the trench is placed a wooden box (or other heavy box), the open end down. This will work better if there are holes or slats in the top (bottom) of the box. Corn kernels or other bird food are then set along the inside of the trench, leading to inside the box. The holes in the top of the box allow light in and produce an illusion of sky, so that when the birds eat their way along the trench and into the box, they will look up when they are finished eating and ready to leave. They then try to fly out up. Three or four birds may be trapped in the box, so it should be checked several times a day. The larger number of boxes, the better the chances of success.

Rotting logs lying on the ground are excellent places to look for a variety of insects, including ants, termites, beetles and grubs, which are beetle larvae. The survivor/evader should not overlook insect nests on or in the ground. Grassy areas, such as fields, are good areas to search because the insects are easily seen. Stones, boards or other materials lying on the ground provide the insects with nesting sites. Insect larvae are also edible. Insects that have a hard outer shell, such as beetles and grasshoppers, will have parasites. Cook them before eating. Remove any wings and barbed legs also.

The soldier can eat most insects raw. The taste varies from one species to another. Wood grubs are bland, while some species of ants store honey in their bodies, giving them a sweet taste. The soldier can grind a collection of insects into a paste, mix them with edible vegetation or cook them to improve their taste.

Worms (Annelidea) are an excellent protein source. The soldier should dig for them in damp humus soil or watch for them on the ground after a rain. After

capturing them, he should drop them into clean, potable water for a few minutes. The worms will naturally purge or wash themselves out, after which they can be eaten raw.

Crustacea

Freshwater shrimp range in size from a 2.5mm (0.1in) up to 2.5cm (1in). They can form rather large colonies in mats of floating algae or in the muddy bottoms of ponds and lakes.

Crayfish are distinguished by their hard exoskeleton and five pairs of legs, the front pair having oversized pincers. Crayfish are active at night, but they are located in the daytime by looking under and around stones in streams. They are also found by looking in the soft mud near the chimney-like breathing holes of their nests. The survivor can catch crayfish by tying bits of offal or internal organs to a string. When the crayfish grabs the bait, it is pulled to shore before it has a chance to release it.

The soldier can find saltwater lobsters, crabs and shrimp from the seashore out to water 10m (32ft) deep. Shrimp may come to a light at night where he can scoop them up with a net. He can also catch lobsters and crabs with a baited trap or a baited hook. Crabs will come to bait placed at the edge of the surf, where they are trapped or netted. Lobsters and crabs are nocturnal and best caught at night.

Molluscs

This class includes octopus and freshwater and saltwater shellfish such as snails, clams, mussels, bivalves, barnacles, periwinkles, chitons and sea urchins. The survivor/evader can find bivalves similar to the North American freshwater mussel and terrestrial and aquatic snails world-wide under all water conditions.

River snails or freshwater periwinkles are plentiful in rivers, streams and lakes of northern coniferous forests. These snails may be pencil point or globular in shape. In fresh water, the soldier looks for molluscs in the shallows, especially in water with a sandy or muddy bottom. He will spot the narrow trails they leave in the mud or the dark elliptical slit of their open valves.

Near the sea he should look in the tidal pools and the wet sand. Rocks along beaches or extending as reefs into deeper water often support clinging shellfish. Snails and limpets cling to rocks and seaweed from the low water mark upward. Large snails, called chitons, adhere tightly to rocks above the surf line.

Mussels usually form dense colonies in or around rock pools, on logs or at the base of boulders.

The escaper/evader should steam, boil or bake molluscs in the shell. Molluscs make excellent stews in combination with vegetables such as greens and tubers. However, the soldier should not eat shellfish that are not covered by water at high tide. He should also beware of mussels in tropical areas, as they can be poisonous in summer.

Fish

Fish represent a good source of protein and fat. They offer some distinct advantages to the soldier engaged in survival or evasion. They are usually more abundant than mammal wildlife, and they can be acquired almost silently. To be successful at catching fish, the soldier must know their habits. For instance, fish tend to feed heavily before a storm. Fish are not likely to feed after a storm when the water is muddy and swollen. Light often attracts fish at night. When there is a heavy current, fish will rest in places where there is an eddy, such as near rocks. Fish will also gather where there are deep pools, under overhanging brush, and in and around submerged foliage, logs or other objects that offer them shelter. The survivor/evader should examine the water and foreshore for life forms like frogs, snails, crayfish and small silvery brown fish. He should select his bait on the basis of what he has observed. For example, a dark or black rubber worm is good for bass or chain pickerel (rubber worms are artificial bait made from the rubber weather seals around doors and windows in buildings and vehicles).

The soldier should make the bait move like a living thing, and wait until he feels a tug on the line. A big fish will swim up and gently grab the bait. The fish will swim until it finds safe haven and then swallow the worm. The soldier must be patient and above all, quiet – sound travels down the line. He watches the line slowly leave the spool. When it stops, the fish has found a place of safety. Once it starts moving again, the fish has swallowed the worm and can be drawn into shore. Hooks can be produced from almost any item made out of steel wire. The wire

Below: A basket trap can take time to make, but is worth the effort. Construct the trap from branches of a tree, forming a tight funnel at one end. Set the trap in a rock channel of a fast-flowing stream or river. Usually, within minutes, the trap can produce a large catch of fish and river creatures.

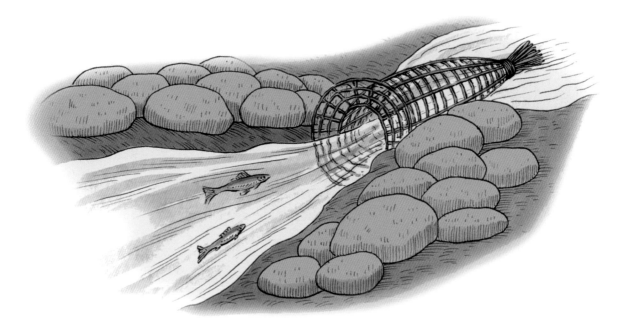

from a spiral-bound note book, toys, vehicle parts, broken electronics units, barbed wire – in fact, a single spiral of any small, steel spring can be fashioned into a hook. One spring can be made into a dozen or more hooks. Sharpen the tip on a file, stone or rock, then carefully bend it into shape.

Almost anything around can be fashioned into a jig or lure: metal from cans (using a nail to punch holes); berries from bushes; buttons from clothing; beads from jewellery; spoons, knives and forks from the kitchen; seasonal ornaments. Chunks of expanded polystyrene packing can be used as floats.

There are no poisonous freshwater fish. However, the catfish species has sharp, needle-like protrusions on its dorsal fins and barbels. These can inflict painful puncture wounds that quickly become infected. The soldier should cook all freshwater fish to kill parasites, the same applying to saltwater fish caught within a reef or within the influence of a freshwater source. Any marine life obtained farther out in the sea will not contain parasites because of the saltwater environment, and these can be eaten raw.

Certain saltwater species of fish have poisonous flesh. In some species, the poison occurs seasonally; in others, it is permanent. Examples of poisonous saltwater fish are the porcupine fish, triggerfish, cowfish, thorn fish, oilfish, red

Below: A US Marine instructor extracts snake venom for the benefit of trainees. Not all snakes are poisonous and are a valuable protein source for a survivor. However, care should be taken when trapping and killing them.

EATING AMPHIBIANS

In some cultures, frogs are regarded as a delicacy and the survivor/evader should not allow inhibitions or squeamishness to deter him from gathering them as food.

Frogs and salamanders are easily found around bodies of fresh water. Frogs seldom move from the safety of the water's edge. At the first sign of danger, they plunge into the water and bury themselves in the mud and debris. There are few poisonous species of frogs. Any that are brightly coloured or have a distinct 'X' mark on the back are best avoided. Toads must be distinguished from frogs. The soldier will normally find toads in drier environments. Several species of toads secrete a poisonous substance through their skin as a defence against attack, so to avoid poisoning, he will not handle or eat toads.

Salamanders are nocturnal. The best time to catch them is at night, using a light. They can range in size from a few centimetres to well over 60cm (24in) in length. The survivor/evader should look in water around rocks and mud banks for salamanders.

snapper, jack and puffer. The barracuda, while not actually poisonous itself, may transmit ciguatera (fish poisoning) if eaten raw.

One plant that is encountered during fishing and which should never be overlooked is seaweed. It is a form of marine algae found on or near ocean shores. There are also some edible freshwater varieties. Seaweed is a valuable source of iodine, other minerals and vitamin C. Large quantities of seaweed in an unaccustomed stomach can produce a severe laxative effect. When gathering seaweed for food, the soldier should choose living plants attached to rocks or floating free. Seaweed washed onshore any length of time may be spoiled. The survivor can dry freshly harvested seaweed for later use. Its preparation for eating depends on the type of seaweed. Thin and tender varieties can be dried in the sun or over a fire until crisp, then crushed and added to soups or broths. Thick, leathery seaweed should be boiled for a short time to soften it. Seaweed is then eaten as a vegetable or with other foods. The most common edible seaweed are Dulse, Green Seaweed, Irish Moss, Kelp, Laver, Mojaban and Sugar Wrack.

Reptiles

Reptiles are a good protein source and relatively easy to catch. They should be cooked, but in an emergency can be eaten raw. Their raw flesh may transmit parasites, but because reptiles are cold-blooded, they do not carry the blood diseases of the warm-blooded animals.

The box turtle is a commonly encountered turtle that should be avoided as a food source. It feeds on poisonous mushrooms and may build up a highly toxic poison in its flesh. Cooking does not destroy this toxin. The survivor/evader should also avoid the hawksbill turtle, found in the Atlantic Ocean, because of its poisonous thorax gland. Poisonous snakes, alligators, crocodiles and large sea turtles present obvious hazards to the survivor. Care should be taken when handling and capturing large freshwater turtles, such as the snapping turtles and soft-shelled turtles of North America and the Matamata and other turtles of South America. All of these turtles will bite in self-defence and can sever fingers and toes.

TOOLS AND WEAPONS

If the survivor/evader does not have a survival kit with knives and tools, he will need to improvise them. The simplest tool is a club that can double as a hammer and weapon. Clubs are held and not thrown. As a field-expedient weapon, the club does not protect the soldier from a human enemy. It can, however, extend his area of defence beyond his fingertips. It also serves to increase the force of a blow. There are three basic types of clubs the simple, weighted and sling club.

A simple club is a staff or branch. It must be short enough for a person to swing easily, but long enough and strong enough for the user to damage whatever he hits. Its diameter should fit comfortably in his hand, but it should not be so thin that it will break easily upon impact. A straight-grained hardwood is ideal.

Right: A British Army combat medical technician cuts branches from a tree to construct a brushwood shelter during a combat survival course in northern Norway, 2001.

A weighted club is any simple club with a weight on one end. This may be natural, such as a knot on the wood, or something added, such as a stone lashed to the club. To make a weighted club, the soldier first finds a stone that has a shape which allows it to be lashed securely to the club. A stone with a slight hourglass shape works well. An alternative is to shape a groove or channel into the stone by a technique known as pecking. By repeatedly rapping the club stone with a smaller hard stone, the desired shape can be achieved. Next he should find a piece of wood that is the right length, again a straight-grained hardwood is best. The length of the wood should feel comfortable in relation to the weight of the stone. Finally, the stone is lashed to the handle.

A sling club is another type of weighted club that uses the principles of a flail. A weight hangs 8–10cm (3–4in) from the handle by a strong, flexible lashing. This type of club both extends the user's reach and multiplies the force of the blow

A more effective weapon and tool is a knife. This can be improvised from a variety of materials – some of the earliest examples of knives to be found in Europe date back to 1800 BC and are made from shaped flint.

A sharp-edged piece of stone, a chipping tool and a flaking tool are required to make a stone knife. The chipping tool is a light, blunt-edged tool used to break off small pieces of stone, while the flaking tool is a pointed tool used to break off thin, flattened pieces of stone. A chipping tool can be made from wood, bone or metal, and a flaking tool from bone, antler tines or soft iron.

MAKING A KNIFE

To start making the knife, the shape is roughed out on the chosen piece of sharp stone, using the chipping tool to make the knife fairly thin. Then, the flaking tool is pressed against the edges. This action will cause flakes to come off the opposite side, leaving a razor sharp edge. Eventually there will be a very sharp cutting edge that can used as a knife, and this is lashed to some type of hilt. Stone will make an excellent puncturing tool and a good chopping tool, but will not hold a fine edge for long.

Bone is an effective field-expedient edged weapon. The larger bones, such as the leg bone of a deer or another medium-sized animal, are best. To make an arrowhead or spearhead, lay the bone upon another hard object. Shatter the bone by hitting it with a heavy object, such as a rock. From the pieces, select a suitable pointed splinter. This splinter can be further shaped and sharpened by rubbing it on a rough-surfaced rock. If the piece is too small to handle, it can still be used by adding a handle to it.

Below: The superb Leatherman Wave – the original idea for a multi-tool developed by Tim Leatherman – has now been copied in many different formats. The Leatherman is still the best and even in its most basic form is a valuable survival tool.

KNIFE SHARPENING

soldier's kit may include a sharpening steel or stone, but if he lacks this equipment he can improvise. The US Air Force survival manual AFM 64-5 includes advice on field-expedient sharpening techniques. Any sandstone will sharpen tools, but a grey, somewhat clayey sandstone gives better results than a pure quartz. Quartz is the only common mineral that will bite into steel, every grain cutting a bright groove into the metal.

If sandstone is not available, the manual recommends using granite or any glittering, crystalline rock except marble. It advises that granite should be rubbed against another piece to produce a smooth surface. SAS survival expert 'Lofty' Wiseman concurs – he advises that to sharpen a knife a clockwise circular motion should be used with steady pressure on the blade with the fingertips of the left hand as it is pushed away. The knife angle should be constant and the stone kept wet. Dragging the blade can produce burrs. For the opposite side of the blade, the sharpening process should be anticlockwise.

Select a suitable piece of hardwood for a handle and lash the bone splinter securely to it.

Knives shaped from wood and bone were favoured by some cultures. Wood was used by the Jivaro Indians of Ecuador to produce a double-ended dagger. Bamboo, however, is the only wood that will hold a suitable edge. To make a knife using wood, the soldier should chose a straight-grained piece of hardwood that is about 30cm (11.8in) long and 250cm (9.8in) in diameter, from which a blade about 15cm (5.9in) long is fashioned. It is shaved down to a point using only the straight-grained portions of the wood and not the core or pith, which would make a weak point.

If it is possible to kindle a fire, the blade portion should be held over the flame until lightly charred. The drier the wood, the harder the point. After lightly charring the blade portion, it can then be sharpened on a coarse stone.

Glass is a good alternative to an edged weapon or tool, if no other material is available. Glass has a natural edge but is less durable for heavy work. Plastic can also be sharpened if it is thick enough or hard enough to form a durable point for puncturing. If the survivor/evader has a conventional steel knife, it will begin to lose its edge with use. Factors like blade thickness, blade shape, edge angle, edge thickness and edge smoothness determine cutting ability.

Blade thickness is set by the manufacturer and determines the blade's slicing ability. A hunting knife will never slice like a fillet knife or a kitchen knife, no matter what is done to the edge. It is possible to change blade thickness a little near the edge, and this can enhance cutting ability. The blade shape reflects the function of the knife, for example: skinning, gutting or cutting tough materials. Like the thickness, the shape is established when the blade is made.

Edge angle, edge thickness and edge smoothness are the factors that can be affected by the user with careful sharpening. Edge angle is measured between the centre of the blade and the bevel, or flat cut, by the stone. Most US and European knives are double bevel, so the total angle at the edge is twice this angle.

Edge angles can vary from 10º to 40º, but most filleting knives are between 15º and survival knives 30º. Different angles are suited for different tasks, so 20º is about right for kitchen knives, 22º is good for pocket knives, and 25º gives a long lasting edge to a camp knife. A good starting point is to duplicate the angle the maker put on the blade. Edge angle is difficult to measure after the fact, but is fairly easy to control when sharpening by controlling the angle between the stone and the blade. Any edge thickness under a few thousandths of an inch may be considered sharp. Paper is about two to three thousandths thick and can cut skin if conditions are right.

Edge thickness naturally increases with wear. It is affected by malleability, or the tendency for steel to move when it is pushed. Steel is strong, but at the edge this strength can be so diminished that it takes only the pressure of a fraction of an ounce to move it. The force of a hand with a stone or steel can move enough steel to create or smooth a burr. The second limit to edge thickness is edge smoothness. The grit of the cutting stone determines scratch pattern or smoothness. Good edge smoothness requires careful work with a very fine stone

The most common way to test an edge is to rub the thumb lightly across the blade or shave hair on the hand or arm. Shaving sharpness can be achieved even on

Above: To make a knife from glass, simply split a stick, insert the glass in the groove and lash it securely.

Left: A sharp knife gives confidence for any task. Here, an instructor demonstrates gutting a rabbit to a survival class, in a brisk operation that quickly turns the animal into edible meat.

heavy hunting knives or an axe. Razor sharpness is only possible with both a polished edge and a small edge angle.

Testing by shaving hairs on the arms or back of the hand can be misleading if the blade has a burr or wire edge. Steel naturally forms a burr – a thin bendable projection on the edge – during the sharpening process. A blade with a burr will shave, but will not stand up to hard use. To test for a burr, fingertips can be slid lightly from the side of the blade over the edge, the burr will drag against the fingers. Burrs are usually bent over one way or the other so both sides should be checked. To see a dull edge, hold the blade with the edge in line with a bright light and move it around. A dull edge will reflect a glint, as will nicks and burrs.

Another test for sharpness is to press the edge lightly on a thumbnail at angle of about 30°. If it cuts into the nail, it is sharp; but if it slips, it is dull.

FIRE

Fire is essential for signalling, heat and cooking, and the survivor must know several methods of creating fires. There are three elements in a fire: air, heat and fuel. If the survivor/evader removes any of these, the fire will go out. The correct ratio of these elements is very important for a fire to burn effectively and the best way to learn the combination of the three is practice.

If the survivor/evader is in a wooded or brush-covered area, he should clear the brush and scrape the surface soil from the spot he has selected at least 1m (3ft) in diameter so there is little chance of the fire spreading. Also, if time allows, he can construct a firewall using logs or rocks. This wall will help to direct the heat where he wants it. It will also reduce flying sparks and cut down on the amount of wind blowing into the fire. However, he will need enough wind (the air element) to keep the fire burning.

The survivor/evader needs three types of materials to build a fire – tinder, kindling and fuel. Tinder is dry, light and fibrous material that ignites with little heat or even just a spark. The tinder must be absolutely dry to be sure just a spark

LOCATION, LOCATION, LOCATION

Before building a fire, the soldier should consider the area (terrain and climate) in which he is operating; the materials and tools available; how much time is available; the need for a fire; and how close is the enemy? He then looks for a suitable spot to build the fire.

A good fire location is one that:
· Is protected from the wind.
· Is suitably placed in relation to his shelter.
· Will concentrate the heat in the direction he desires.
· Has a supply of wood or other fuel available.

will ignite it, and examples include dried grasses, pocket fluff and the linings from birds' nests. Charred cloth is also an excellent tinder, made by heating cotton cloth until it turns black but does not burn. Once it is black, the soldier must keep it in an airtight container to keep it dry.

Kindling is readily combustible material that is added to the burning tinder, ideally small dry sticks. Again, this material should be absolutely dry to ensure rapid burning. Kindling increases the fire's temperature so that it will ignite less combustible material – fuel. Fuel is any material that burns slowly and steadily once ignited, and generates large amounts of heat – typically logs or coals. When lighting any fire, the tinder is first ignited, then the kindling added slowly (without smothering the fire) until the heat and flames are raised, and finally the main fuel is put on to establish the fire. To ignite a fire, the survivor can rely on either modern or traditional igniters.

Left: A Territorial Army trooper with 21 SAS cooks a rabbit over an open fire around last light. If fires are kept burning after dark, they will need to be carefully screened from hostile search parties.

Modern Igniters

The most obvious igniters for fires are matches. These should be waterproof and windproof and stored in a waterproof container along with a dependable striker pad. Some survival specialists favour the red no-safety matches that can be struck on any abrasive surface. Gas or petrol lighters are useful since they generate a sustained strong flame.

The convex lens method of ignition can be used only on bright, sunny days. The lens might come from binoculars, a camera, a telescopic sight or a magnifying glass. It is angled into the sun to concentrate the sun's rays on the tinder, and is held over the same spot until the tinder begins to smoulder. As it smoulders, the soldier gently blows or fans the tinder to encourage a flame.

The metal match – a high-grade piece of flint – is a classic item of survival kit. To use the metal match, a flat, dry leaf is placed under the tinder with a portion exposed. The tip of the metal match is placed on the leaf, holding the metal match in one hand and a knife in the other. When the knife is scraped down the metal match, it produces a shower of sparks, igiting the tinder, which can then be fanned or blown gently into a flame.

The soldier can also use a battery to generate a spark, depending on the type of battery available. Ideally, the battery should be a vehicle battery or powerful torch battery to generate the necessary current. A wire is attached to each terminal, and the ends of the bare wires touched together next to the tinder to make sparks.

The military survivor/evader will often have ammunition with his equipment.

Right: The drill technique for making fire can be hard on the hands and requires patience and application. Friction from the drilling action builds up enough heat to ignite the tinder that has been placed in the slot in the block of wood.

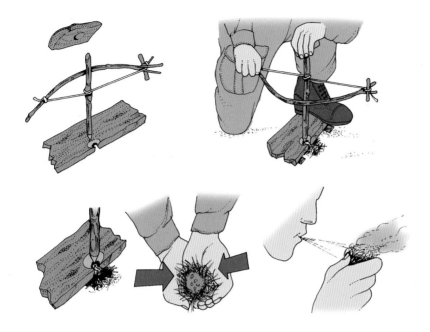

If so, he can carefully extract the bullet from the shell casing, and use the gunpowder as tinder. A spark will ignite the powder. However, he should be extremely careful when extracting the bullet from the case.

Traditional Igniters

Traditional igniters were used by our early ancestors and tribes in remote parts of the world. They require patience and hard work to be effective.

The direct spark method from a flint and steel is the easiest of the primitive methods to use. The soldier strikes a flint or other hard, sharp-edged rock edge with a piece of carbon steel (stainless steel will not produce a good spark). This method requires a loose-jointed wrist and practice. When a spark has caught in the tinder, it is fanned into a flame.

The fire-plough is a friction method of ignition. The soldier rubs a hardwood shaft against a softer wood base. To use this method, he cuts a straight groove in the base and ploughs the blunt tip of the shaft up and down the groove. The ploughing action of the shaft pushes out small particles of wood fibres. Then, as he applies more pressure on each stroke, the friction ignites the wood particles.

The technique of starting a fire with a bow and drill is simple, but the soldier must exert much effort and be persistent to produce a fire. He needs the following items to use this method:

Socket – The socket is an easily grasped stone or piece of hardwood or bone with a slight depression in one side. It is used to hold the drill in place and to apply downward pressure.

Drill – The drill should be a straight, seasoned hardwood stick about 2cm (0.7in)

Below: A tepee fire is a good basic campfire because it is easy to make, and the structure serves to encourage a good flow of air to get the flames rising. Build the fire in a square section of earth, laying a base of tinder (A) to give the fire stability. Now construct the tepee, first fixing timber in the four corners to provide the tepee shape (B). Complete the kindling structure (C), leaving an opening around the bases for tinder to be inserted. Finally, insert the tinder just outside the tepee, and push it into the structure (D). The structure offers numerous paths for the fire to work its way up.

in diameter and 25cm (10in) long. The top end is round and the low end blunt (to produce more friction).

Fire board – Its size is up to the individual. A seasoned softwood board about 2.5cm (1in) thick and 10cm (4in) wide is preferable. A depression about 2cm (0.7in) wide is cut from the edge on one side of the board. On the underside, a V-shaped notch is cut from the edge of the board to the depression.

Bow – The bow is a resilient, green stick about 2.5cm (1in) in diameter fitted with a string to make a bow configuration. The type of wood is not important. The bowstring can be any type of cordage. The survivor/evader ties the bowstring from one end of the bow to the other, without any slack.

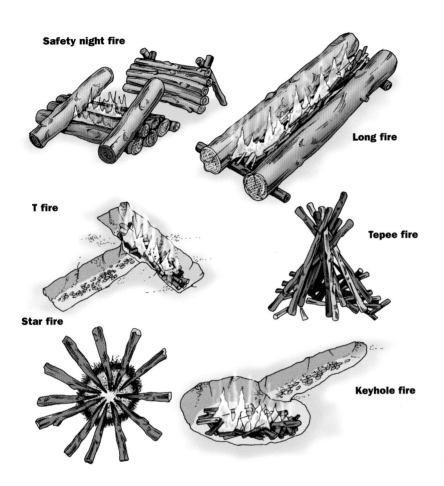

Safety night fire

Long fire

T fire

Tepee fire

Star fire

Keyhole fire

Left: Different types of fire produce different burn characteristics. Remember that the more open the fire's structure, the more air is introduced, and the more intensely the fire will burn.

FIRE TYPES

If it is safe to build a fire, the soldier should locate it well away from the hide site and camouflage and sterilize the site after each use. He must be careful that smoke and light from the fire does not compromise the hole-up area. Opinions vary as to exactly when it is safe enough to light a fire. However, sometimes it is crucial to purify food or water by cooking or boiling, or to provide warmth to prevent hypothermia. If the situation permits he should bank the fire up with coals to keep it in overnight – however, he should be sure that it extinguished when he leaves.

In some situations, he may find that an underground or 'Dakota' fireplace will best meet his needs. It conceals the fire and serves well for cooking food. He digs a fire pit deep enough to hide the flames, with a separate airshaft at an angle to the pit – this will make the fire burn quicker and prevent excessive smoke. If the ground is too hard to dig, is too waterlogged, or a fire pit is impractical for some other reason, the fire can be lit under a canopy of leafy foliage to disperse smoke. Alternatively, the fire can be positioned against a high wall. He should try to ensure that flames do not show above ground.

Above: The fire burning in this jungle shelter is not only protected from the rain, but will keep insects and even larger animals at bay.

If he is in a snow-covered area, several green logs placed side by side on top of the snow make a dry base for the fire (never wet or porous stones, as these may explode when heated). Trees with wrist-sized trunks are easily broken in extreme cold

To make a Tepee Fire, he should arrange the tinder and a few sticks of kindling in the shape of a tepee or cone before lighting a fire in the centre. As the tepee burns, the outside logs will fall inward, feeding the fire. This type of fire burns well even with wet wood.

To lay the Lean-To Fire, the soldier pushes a green stick into the ground at a an angle of 30° and points the end of the stick in the direction of the wind. Tinder is placed deep under this lean-to stick and pieces of kindling put against against the lean-to stick. As the kindling catches fire from the tinder, more kindling is added.

To use the Cross-Ditch Fire, he scratches a cross about 30cm (12in) wide and 7.5cm (3in) deep in the ground, placing a large wad of tinder in the middle of the cross. A kindling pyramid is built above the tinder. The shallow ditch allows air to sweep under the tinder to provide a draft.

To lay the Pyramid Fire, the soldier places two small logs or branches parallel on the ground and a solid layer of small logs across the parallel logs. Three or four more layers of logs or branches are added, each layer smaller than and at a right angle to the layer below it. He makes a starter fire on top of the pyramid. As the starter fire burns, it will ignite the logs below it. This gives the survivor/evader a fire that burns downward, requiring no attention during the night.

In addition to basic survival skills, the modern soldier is also trained in the survival skills of extreme environments, typically tropical, arctic and desert. Each of these environments presents distinct survival challenges.

TROPICAL SURVIVAL

High temperatures, heavy rainfall and oppressive humidity characterize equatorial and subtropical regions, except at high altitudes. In jungle terrain, dense growth limits visibility to about 50m (164ft) and less, and the survivor/evader can easily lose his sense of direction, and it is extremely hard for rescue aircraft to see him. He will probably have to travel to reach safety.

If he has been shot down or is the victim of an aircraft crash, the most important items for him to take from the crash site are a machete, a compass, a first-aid kit and a parachute or other material for use as mosquito netting and shelter. He should pinpoint his initial location as accurately as possible to determine a general line of travel to safety. If he does not have a compass, he should use a field-expedient direction-finding method.

With practice, movement through thick undergrowth and jungle can be done efficiently. To move easily, the soldier should develop a 'jungle eye': he should not

FINDING WATER IN THE JUNGLE

Even though water is abundant in most tropical environments, a soldier may have trouble finding it. If he does find water, it may not be safe to drink. Some of the many tropical water sources are vines, roots, palm trees and condensation. The survivor/evader can sometimes follow animals (particularly grazing animals), trails of ants and flying birds to water. Often he can produce nearly clear water from muddy streams or lakes by digging a hole in sandy soil about 1m (3ft) from the bank. Water will seep into the hole. He must purify any water obtained in this manner.

Human tracks will usually lead to a well, bore hole or soak. Scrub or rocks may cover it to reduce evaporation. The survivor/evader should replace the cover after use. Vines with rough bark and shoots about 5cm (2in) thick can be a useful source of water. The survivor/evader must learn by experience which are the water-bearing vines, because not all have drinkable

water. The poisonous ones yield a sticky, milky sap when cut. Non-poisonous vines will give a clear fluid. Some vines cause a skin irritation on contact; therefore the survivor/evader should let the liquid drip into his mouth, rather than put his mouth to the vine. He should preferably use some type of container.

The buri, coconut and nipa palms all contain a sugary fluid that is very good to drink. To obtain the liquid, he bends a flowering stalk of one of these palms downward, and cuts off its tip. If he cuts a thin slice off the stalk every 12 hours, the flow will renew, making it possible to collect up to 1 litre (1.8 pints) per day. Nipa palm shoots grow from the base, so the soldier can work at ground level. On grown trees of other species, he may have to climb them to reach a flowering stalk. Coconut milk has a large water content, but may contain a strong laxative in ripe nuts. Drinking too much of this milk may cause him to lose more fluid than he drinks.

concentrate on the pattern of bushes and trees immediately to his front, but focus on the jungle further out and find natural breaks in the foliage. Look through the jungle, not at it.

In enemy territory, he takes advantage of natural cover and concealment. He stays alert and moves slowly and steadily through dense forest or jungle, stopping periodically to listen and take his bearings. A machete is used to cut through dense vegetation, but he must avoid cutting unnecessarily or he will quickly wear himself out. He should stroke upward when cutting vines to reduce noise, as sound carries long distances in the jungle. He should also use a stick to part the vegetation – this will also help dislodge biting ants, spiders or snakes – and he should not grasp at brush or vines when climbing slopes; they may have irritating spines or sharp thorns. His aim should be to move smoothly through the jungle – not blunder through it, since he will get many cuts and scratches. Movement is aided by turning his shoulders, shifting his hips, bending his body and adjusting his stride as necessary to slide between the undergrowth. He must always wear long sleeves to avoid cuts and scratches.

Many jungle and forest animals follow game trails. These trails wind and cross, but frequently lead to water or clearings. A soldier can use these trails if they lead in the desired direction of travel. In many countries, electric and telephone lines run for miles through sparsely inhabited areas. Usually, the right-of-way is clear enough to allow easy travel. When travelling along these lines, the soldier should be careful as he approaches transformer and relay stations. In enemy territory, they may be guarded.

The jungle climate is aggressive, and the soldier on the run should take shelter from tropical rain, sun and insects. Malaria-carrying mosquitoes and other insects are immediate dangers, so he should protect himself against bites with insect repellent and clothing.

If he is in friendly or neutral territory, he should not leave a crash area without carefully blazing or marking his route. He should use his compass so that he knows what direction he is taking. Health care is also vital. In the tropics, even the smallest scratch can quickly become dangerously infected, so he must promptly treat any wound, no matter how minor.

EDIBLE TROPICAL PLANTS

Edible tropical plants and fruits include Bael fruit, Bamboo (various species), Banana or Plantain, Bignay, Breadfruit, Coconut palm, Fishtail Palm, Horseradish Tree, Lotus, Mango, Manioc, Nipa Palm, Papaya, Persimmon, Rattan Palm, Sago palm, Sterculia, Sugarcane, Sugar Palm, Sweetsop, Taro, Water Lily, Wild Fig, Wild Rice and Yam.

Food

Food is usually abundant in a tropical survival situation. In addition to animal food, the survivor/evader will have to supplement his diet with edible plants. The best places to forage are the banks of streams and rivers. Wherever the sun penetrates the jungle, there will be a mass of vegetation, but riverbanks may be the most accessible areas.

If the survivor/evader is physically weak, he should not expend energy climbing or felling a tree for food. There are more easily obtained sources of food nearer the ground. The survivor should not pick more food than he needs. Food spoils rapidly in tropical conditions. He should leave food on the growing plant until he needs it, and eat it fresh.

There are an almost unlimited number of edible plants from which to choose. Unless the survivor/evader can positively identify these plants, it may be safer at first to begin with palms, bamboos and common fruits.

ARCTIC SURVIVAL

Cold regions include arctic and sub-arctic areas and areas immediately adjoining them. About 48 per cent of the northern hemisphere's total landmass is a cold region due to the influence and extent of air temperatures. Ocean currents affect cold weather and cause large areas normally included in the temperate zone to fall within the cold regions during winter periods. Elevation also has a marked effect on defining cold regions.

It is more difficult for a survivor/evader to satisfy his basic water, food and shelter needs in a cold environment than in a warm environment. Even if he has the basic requirements, he must also have adequate protective clothing and a strong will to survive.

There are many different items of cold-weather equipment and clothing issued to NATO forces today. Specialized units may have access to newer, lightweight gear such as polypropylene underwear, breathable waterproof outerwear and boots, and other special equipment. The survivor/evader should remember, however, that older gear will keep him warm as long as he applies a few cold-weather principles. If the newer types of clothing are available, he should use them. If not, then clothing should be entirely wool, with the possible exception of a windbreaker.

The survivor/evader must not only have enough clothing to protect him from the cold, he must also know how to maximize the warmth he can get from it. For example, the head, is always kept covered. He can lose 40–

Below: When using a transpiration bag, try to keep the vegetation from pressing against the sides of the plastic so that the wood and leaves do not reabsorb the water as it runs down the plastic.

45 per cent of body heat from an unprotected head. The brain is very susceptible to cold and can stand the least amount of cooling. Because there is much blood circulation in the head, most of which is on the surface, he can lose heat quickly if he does not cover his head, and even more heat will be lost from unprotected neck, wrist and ankles.

There are four basic principles to follow to keep warm. An easy way to remember these basic principles is to use the word COLD:

C - Keep clothing clean.

O - Avoid overheating.

L - Wear clothes loose and in layers.

D - Keep clothing dry.

C - Keep clothing clean. This principle is always important for sanitation and comfort. In winter, it is also important from the standpoint of warmth. Clothes matted with dirt and grease lose much of their insulation value. Heat can escape more easily from the body through the clothing's crushed or filled-up air pockets.

O - Avoid overheating. When the soldier gets too hot, he will sweat and his clothing will absorb the moisture. This affects warmth in two ways: dampness decreases the insulating quality of clothing, and as sweat evaporates, his body cools.

He should adjust his clothing so he does not sweat. He does this by partially opening his parka or jacket, by removing an inner layer of clothing, by removing heavy outer mittens, or by throwing back his parka hood or changing to lighter headgear. The head and hands act as efficient heat dissipaters when overheated.

L - Wear clothing loose and in layers. Wearing tight clothing and footgear restricts blood circulation and invites cold injury. It also decreases the volume of air trapped between the layers, reducing its insulating value. Several layers of lightweight clothing are better than one equally thick layer of clothing, because the layers have dead-air space between them. The dead-air space is warmed and provides extra insulation. Also, layers of clothing allow him to take off or add clothing layers to prevent excessive sweating or to increase warmth.

D - Keep clothing dry. In cold temperatures, inner layers of clothing can become wet from sweat and the

Below: The heat from the fire is sufficient to melt snow heaped up in the cloth bag, but not burn the fabric. The melted snow is collected in the container. More snow can be added as it melts to produce a sustained supply of drinking water.

outer layer, if not water repellent, can become wet from snow and frost melted by body heat. The survivor/evader should wear water-repellent outer clothing, if available. It will shed most of the water collected from melting snow and frost. Before entering a heated shelter, he must brush off the snow and frost. Despite the precautions he takes, there will be times when he cannot keep from getting wet. At such times, drying his clothing may become a major problem. On the march, he should hang his damp mittens and socks on his rucksack. Sometimes in freezing temperatures, the wind and sun will dry this clothing. The survivor/evader can also place damp socks or mittens, unfolded, near his body so that his body heat can dry them. In a campsite, he hangs damp clothing inside the shelter near the top, using drying lines or improvised racks. The soldier may even be able to dry each item by holding it before an open fire. He should dry leather items slowly. If no other means are available for drying boots, he can put them between his sleeping bag shell and liner. His body heat will help to dry the leather.

Above: Lance Bombardier Nathan Goodger from 29 Commando Regiment RA shows the equipment required for a soldier to survive and fight in Arctic conditions. The photograph was taken in Norway in 2001.

A heavy, down-lined sleeping bag is a valuable piece of survival gear in cold weather, but the down must be kept remains dry. If wet, it loses a lot of its insulation value. An improvised sleeping bag can be made out of parachute cloth or similar material and natural dry material, such as leaves, pine needles or moss – the dry material is placed between two layers of the cloth or fabric.

Extremely hazardous conditions exist when wind and low temperature combine.

Wind chill is the effect of moving air on exposed flesh. For instance, with a 28km/h (17mph) wind and a temperature of -10°C (14°F), the equivalent wind chill temperature is -23°C (-9.4°F). During such conditions, it is imperative that the soldier find or make shelter to get out of the wind. At its most basic, the arctic shelter might simply be a small cave dug out of deep snowdrift.

COLD INJURIES

The most dangerous threat to a survivor in arctic conditions is hypothermia. Hypothermia is the lowering of the body temperature at a rate faster than the body can produce heat. Causes of hypothermia may be general exposure to cold or the sudden wetting of the body by, for example, falling into a lake.

The initial symptom is shivering. The shivering may progress to the point that it is uncontrollable and interferes with an individual's ability to care for himself. This begins when the body's core temperature falls to about 35.5°C (96°F). When

Below: British Royal Marines from the Brigade Patrol Troop (Mountain and Arctic Warfare Cadre) 3 Commando Brigade man a covert observation post in Norway. The white face masks provide both camouflage and protection in the bitter weather.

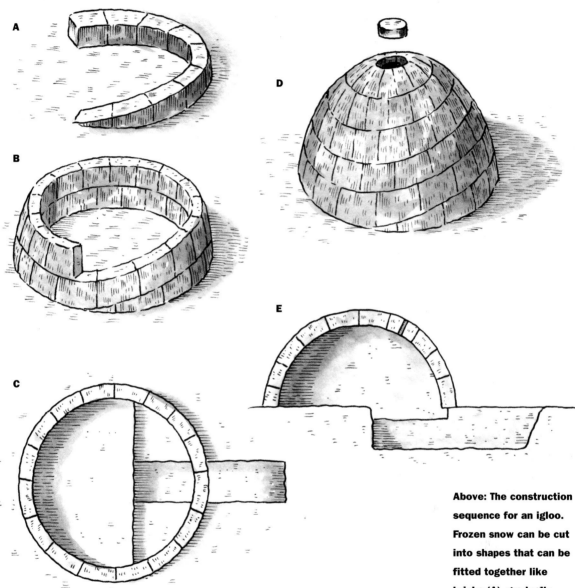

the core temperature reaches 35–32°C (95–90°F), sluggish thinking, irrational reasoning and a false feeling of warmth may occur. Core temperatures of 32–30° C (90–86°F) and below result in muscle rigidity, unconsciousness and barely detectable signs of life. If the victim's core temperature falls below 25°C (77°F), death is almost certain.

To treat hypothermia, the entire body needs to be warmed. If there are means available, the soldier should warm the person by first immersing the trunk area

Above: The construction sequence for an igloo. Frozen snow can be cut into shapes that can be fitted together like bricks (A), gradually building up the levels in a circular design (B). Like the snow hole (see page 153), access is through a trench (see C and E) in which cold air is trapped and there is no opening through which the wind can blow.

TRENCH FOOT AND IMMERSION FOOT

Trench Foot and Immersion Foot result from the feet being exposed to many hours or days of wet or damp conditions at a temperature just above freezing. The symptoms are a sensation of pins and needles, tingling, numbness and then pain. The skin will initially appear wet, soggy, white and shrivelled. As it progresses and damage appears, the skin will take on a red and then a bluish or black discoloration. The feet become cold, swollen and have a waxy appearance. Walking becomes difficult and the feet feel heavy and numb. The nerves and muscles sustain the main damage, but gangrene can occur. In extreme cases, the flesh dies and it may become necessary to have the foot or leg amputated. The best prevention is to keep feet dry, the soldier carrying extra socks in a waterproof packet. Wet socks can be dried against the torso (back or chest). Each day, the feet should be washed and dry socks put on.

only in warm water of 37.7–43.3° C (100–110°F). Warming the whole body in a warm water bath should be done only in hospital because of the increased risk of cardiac arrest and re-warming shock.

One of the quickest ways to get heat to the inner core is to give warm water enemas. Such an action, however, may not be possible in a survival situation. Another method is to wrap the victim in a warm sleeping bag with another person who is already warm; both should be naked. However, the individual placed in the sleeping bag with the victim could also become a hypothermia victim if left in too long.

If the victim is conscious, he should be given hot, sweetened fluids. One of the best sources of calories is honey or dextrose; if unavailable, sugar, cocoa or a similar soluble sweetener can be used. However, an unconscious person must never be forced to drink.

There are two dangers in treating hypothermia, re-warming too rapidly and 'after drop'. Re-warming too rapidly can cause the victim to have circulatory problems, resulting in heart failure. 'After drop' is the sharp body core temperature drop that occurs when taking the victim from the warm water. Its probable cause is the return of previously stagnant limb blood to the core (inner torso) area as recirculation occurs. Concentrating on warming the core area and stimulating peripheral circulation will lessen the effects of after drop.

Frostbite is the result of frozen tissues. With light frostbite, the skin only takes on a dull whitish pallor. Deep frostbite extends to a depth below the skin. The tissues become solid and immovable. Feet, hands and exposed facial areas are particularly vulnerable to frostbite.

The best frostbite prevention is simply to cover up exposed areas with dry, warm clothing. When the survivor/evader is with others, he can use the buddy system to spot whitening areas of flesh. If he is alone, he should periodically cover his nose and the lower part of his face with his mittened hand.

The following pointers will aid the soldier in keeping warm and preventing frostbite:
• Face. Maintain circulation by twitching and wrinkling the skin on face and making faces. Warm with his hands.
• Ears. Wiggle and move ears. Warm with hands.
• Hands. Move hands inside gloves. Warm by placing hands close to the body or under armpits.
• Feet. Move feet and wiggle toes inside boots.

A loss of feeling in the hands and feet is a sign of frostbite. If the survivor/evader has lost feeling for only a short time, the frostbite is probably light. Otherwise, he must assume the frostbite is deep. To re-warm a light frostbite, he uses hands or mittens to warm the face and ears, places hands under his armpits or places feet next to a partner's stomach. A deep frostbite injury, if thawed and then allowed to refreeze, will cause more damage than a non-medically trained person can handle.

When dressed in many layers of clothing, the survivor/evader may be unaware that he is losing body moisture even in cold weather. Heavy clothing absorbs the moisture that evaporates in the air. He must drink water to replace this loss of fluid. The need for water is as great in a cold environment as it is in a warm one. One way that a soldier can tell if he is becoming dehydrated is to check the colour of his urine on snow. If urine makes the snow dark yellow, he is becoming dehydrated and needs to replace body fluids. If it makes the snow light yellow to no colour, his body fluids have a more normal balance.

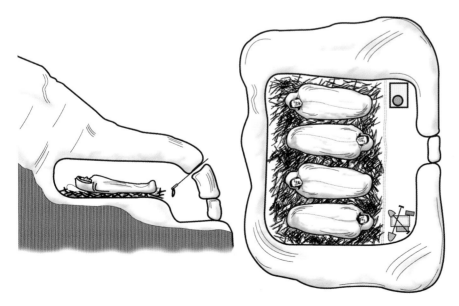

Left: The snow hole dug out of a drift on the side of a hill or cutting has a sleeping platform above the cold air at the entrance. A ski stick is stuck through the roof to provide air and allow rescuers to spot the location.

Exposure to cold increases urine output, although it is very important that the survivor/evader should relieve himself when needed. He should not delay because of the cold. This delay, along with eating dehydrated foods, drinking too little liquid and irregular eating habits, can give him constipation. Although not disabling, it can cause some discomfort. The survivor/evader should increase his fluid intake to at least 2 litres (3.5 pints) above his normal 2–3 litres (3.5–5 litres) daily intake and, if available, eat fruit and other foods that will loosen the stool.

As winter sports enthusiasts know, exposed skin can become sunburned even when the air temperature is below freezing. The sun's rays reflect at all angles from snow, ice and water, hitting sensitive areas of skin, the lips, nostrils and eyelids. Exposure to the sun results in sunburn more quickly at high altitudes than at low altitudes. The survivor/evader should apply sunburn cream or lip salve to his face when in the sun.

Right: As dusk approaches, a British Commando collects brushwood and tree branches to make a fire and shelter during training in northern Norway. Survival training like this is essential in preparing combatants for potential survival situations.

The reflection of the sun's ultraviolet rays off a snow-covered area can cause snow blindness. The symptoms are a sensation of grit in the eyes, pain in and over the eyes that increases with eyeball movement, red and teary eyes, and a headache that intensifies with continued exposure to light. Prolonged exposure to these rays can result in permanent eye damage. To treat snow blindness, eyes should be bandaged until the symptoms disappear.

The soldier can prevent snow blindness by wearing sunglasses. If he does not have sunglasses, he can improvise them by cutting slits in a piece of cardboard, thin wood, tree bark or other available material. Putting soot under his eyes will also help reduce shine and glare.

DESERT SURVIVAL

One of the toughest environments in which to survive is the desert. Surviving and evading the enemy in an arid area depends on what the soldier knows and how prepared he is for the environmental conditions he will face. He should determine what equipment he will need, the tactics he will use, and the environment's impact on them and him.

Above: To make snow shoes, find two flexible saplings, and trim them of any branches (A). Bend the sapling into a balloon shape and knot the two ends firmly together (B). Tie double cross members across the shoe frame, using short stout sticks (C). These cross-members should brace the foot at the ball, arch and heel (D). Add support struts as necessary, and tie the shoe to the foot.

In a desert area there are seven environmental factors that he must consider:
• Low rainfall.
• Intense sunlight and heat.
• Wide temperature range.
• Sparse vegetation.
• High mineral content near ground surface.
• Sandstorms.
• Mirages.

Low rainfall is the most obvious environmental factor in an arid area. Some desert areas receive less than 10cm (4in) of rain annually, and this rain comes in brief torrents that quickly run off the ground surface. The survivor/evader cannot survive long without water in high desert temperatures. In a desert survival situation, he must first consider 'How much water do I have?' and 'Where are other water sources?'

Intense sunlight and heat are present in all arid areas. Air temperature can rise as high as 60°C (140°F) during the day. Heat gain results from direct sunlight, hot blowing winds, reflective heat (the sun's rays bouncing off the sand) and conductive heat from direct contact with the desert sand and rock. The temperature of desert sand and rock averages 16–22°C (30–40°F), more than that of the air. For instance, when the air temperature is 43°C (110°F), the sand temperature may be 60°C (140°F).

Intense sunlight and heat also increase the body's need for water. To conserve his body fluids and energy, the survivor/evader will need to find shelter to reduce his exposure to the heat of the day. He should travel at night to lessen his use of water. Radios and sensitive items of equipment will also malfunction if exposed to direct desert sunlight.

Although temperatures in arid areas may get as high as 60°C (140°F) during the day, at night they can drop as low as 10°C during the night. The drop in temperature at night occurs rapidly and will chill a person who lacks warm clothing and is unable to move about. The cool evenings and nights are the best times to work or travel. If the survivor/evader's plan is to rest at night, he will find a wool sweater, long underwear and a wool stocking cap extremely helpful.

Vegetation is sparse in arid areas, so a soldier on the run will therefore have trouble finding shelter and camouflaging his movements. During daylight hours, large areas of terrain are visible and easily controlled by a small opposing force. If travelling in hostile territory, he should follow these principles of desert camouflage:
• Hide or seek shelter in dry washes (wadis) with thicker growths of vegetation and cover from oblique observation.
• Use the shadows cast from brush, rocks or outcropping.
• Screen objects that will reflect the light from the sun.

Before moving, the soldier should survey the area for sites that provide cover and concealment. He will have trouble estimating distance. The emptiness of desert terrain causes most people to underestimate distance by a factor of three: What appears to be 1km (0.6 miles) away is really 3km (2 miles) away.

All arid regions have areas where the surface soil has a high mineral content (borax, salt, alkali and lime). Material in contact with this soil wears out quickly, and water in these areas is extremely hard and undrinkable. Wetting the uniform in such water to cool off may cause a skin rash. The Great Salt Lake area in Utah is an example of this type of mineral-laden water and soil. There is little or no plant life, and so shelter is hard to find. These areas are best avoided if possible.

Below: British Royal Marines on a SERE exercise construct a simple shelter in the Omani desert. The ideal material for a shelter in these conditions is a poncho liner since it offers greater thermal protection.

CLIMATIC PHENOMENA IN THE DESERT

Sandstorms occur frequently in most deserts. The greatest danger is getting lost in a swirling wall of sand. The survivor/evader should wear goggles and cover his mouth and nose with cloth. If natural shelter is unavailable, he should mark his direction of travel, lie down and sit out the storm. Dust and wind-blown sand interfere with radio transmissions. Therefore he should be ready to use other means for signalling, such as pyrotechnics, signal mirrors or marker panels, if available.

Mirages are optical phenomena caused by the refraction of light through heated air rising from a sandy or stony surface. They occur in the interior of the desert about 10km (6 miles) from the coast. They make objects at a distance of 1.5km (0.9 miles) or more appear to move. The mirage effect makes it hard for a person to identify targets, estimate range and see objects clearly. However, if he can reach high ground (3m/10ft or more above the desert floor), he can get above the superheated air close to the ground and overcome the mirage effect. Mirages make land navigation difficult because they obscure natural features. The survivor/evader can survey the area at dawn, dusk or by moonlight when there is little likelihood of mirage.

Light levels in desert areas are more intense than in other geographic areas. Moonlit nights are usually crystal clear, winds die down, haze and glare disappear, and visibility is excellent. The survivor/evader can see lights, red flashlights and blackout lights at great distances. Sound carries very far. Conversely, during nights with little moonlight, visibility is extremely poor. Travelling is extremely hazardous. The survivor/evader must avoid getting lost, falling into ravines or stumbling into enemy positions. Movement during such a night is practical only if he has a compass and has spent the day in a shelter, resting, observing and memorizing the terrain, and selecting his route.

Water

Because of the desert's extreme temperatures, it is vital that the soldier in such environments implements strict water preservation procedures and maintains a high water intake. Water conservation measures include (in addition to those outlined earlier in the chapter):

• Finding shade and getting out of the sun.
• Placing insulation between himself and the hot ground.
• Restricting movement.
• Conserving sweat.
• Wearing his complete uniform, including T-shirt. He rolls the sleeves down, covers the head, and protects the neck with a scarf or other item. This protects the body from hot-blowing winds and the direct rays of the sun. The clothing also absorbs sweat, keeping it against the skin to give him its full cooling effect.

• Staying in the shade quietly, fully clothed, not talking, keeping his mouth closed, and breathing through his nose all dramatically reduce the water requirement.

In terms of water intake, at temperatures below 38°C (100°F) the soldier should drink 500ml (1 pint) of water every hour. At temperatures above 38°C (100°F), he should drink 1 litre (1.75 pints) of water every hour. Drinking water at regular intervals helps the body remain cool and decreases sweating. Even when the water supply is low, sipping water constantly will keep the body cooler and reduce water loss through sweating. The soldier should conserve fluids by reducing activity during the heat of day. It is essential that the survivor/evader should not ration water: if he does, he stands a good chance of becoming a heat casualty.

Heat Injuries

Heat injuries range from mild dehydration to life-threatening heat-stroke. Loss of salt due to excessive sweating causes heat cramps. Symptoms are moderate to severe muscle cramps in legs, arms or abdomen. They may start as a mild muscular discomfort, but the soldier should stop all activity, find shade and drink water. If he fails to recognize the early symptoms and continues his physical activity, he will have severe muscle cramps and pain. He should be treated as for heat exhaustion.

Left: The survivor/ evader should never rely on thirst as a guide to water consumption. If he is feeling thirsty, he is already starting to dehydrate and may become a heat casualty.

Above: To extract water from a cactus plant, first slice off the top of the cactus (A), then mash the interior flesh into a pulp (B). Once this is done, insert a hollow reed to drink directly from the cactus (C).

A large loss of body water and salt causes heat exhaustion. The symptoms are headache, mental confusion, irritability, excessive sweating, weakness, dizziness, cramps, and pale, moist, cold (clammy) skin. Move the victim under shade immediately and make him lie on a stretcher or similar item about 45cm (18in) off the ground. Loosen his clothing. Sprinkle him with water and fan him. Have him drink small amounts of water every three minutes. Ensure he stays quiet and rests. Heat-stroke is a severe heat injury caused by extreme loss of water and salt and the body's inability to cool itself. The patient may die if not cooled immediately. Symptoms are a lack of sweat, hot and dry skin, headache, dizziness, fast pulse, nausea and vomiting, and mental confusion leading to unconsciousness. As with heat exhaustion, move the person immediately to shade and lay him on a stretcher about 45cm (18in) off the ground and loosen clothing. Pour water on him (it does not matter if the water is polluted or brackish) and fan him. Massage his arms, legs, and body. If he regains consciousness, let him drink small amounts of water every three minutes.

Survival skills will keep a soldier or airman alive while on the run from the enemy. However, his ultimate goal is not just to stay alive, but to reach home and cross back to friendly lines.

DANGEROUS DESERT ANIMALS

There are several hazards unique to desert survival. Insects of almost every type abound in the desert, and occupied and deserted buildings, ruins and caves are favourite habitats of lice, mites, wasps, flies, spiders, scorpions and centipedes. These areas provide protection from the elements and also attract other wildlife. The survivor/evader should take extra care when staying in such places. He should try to wear gloves at all times and should not place his hands anywhere without first looking to see what is there. He should visually inspect an area before sitting or lying down. When he gets up in the morning, he should shake out and inspect boots and clothing.

All desert areas have snakes. They inhabit ruins, native villages, garbage dumps, caves and rock overhangs that offer shade. The

Above: The scorpion is one of the most obvious hazards in the desert; others include flies, mosquitoes and snakes. Cool damp areas like the underside of rocks are a likely habitat.

survivor/evader should never go barefoot or walk through these areas without carefully inspecting them for snakes. He should pay attention to where he places his feet and hands. Most snakebites result from stepping on or handling snakes. If the soldier sees a snake, he should give it a wide berth.

CHAPTER 7

The Home Run

The critical point of an escape and evasion manoeuvre is the crossing over into friendly lines. It is a moment of great danger, as the frontline is a dangerous place, watched by the enemy and nervous friendly forces.

A key factor affecting the ability to navigate in the home run is that virtually all movement will be done at night. The important use of terrain features as 'handrails' for navigation cannot be underestimated. By carefully observing terrain (riverbeds, ridgelines) during daylight hours, the evader will be able to improve his navigation during hours of darkness. He may also establish the true line of a national boundary and where the fences and barriers are located. During the Cold War, the watch towers and fences of the 'Iron Curtain' were actually within East Germany and the real border was several hundred metres to the west. Some East German evaders who had passed through the fences, ploughed strip and minefields assumed they were in the West, and some even 'surrendered' in ignorance to East German border patrols.

Establishing contact with friendly sentries or patrols is the most crucial part of movement and return to safety. All the soldier's patience, planning and the hardship he has endured will be in vain if he does not exercise caution when contacting friendly frontline forces. Friendly patrols have killed isolated personnel operating behind enemy lines because of ineffective contact procedures. Most of the casualties could have been avoided if caution had been exercised and a few

Left: An effective search and rescue operations (SAR) tool, here a Royal Air Force Wessex helicopter hovers close to cliffs to recover an injured man.

Above: A Russian watchtower looms in the setting sun on the Finnish border. In the Soviet era, these watchtowers were manned by KGB border troops and were equipped with powerful tripod mounted marine binoculars and radios.

simple rules followed. The normal tendency is to throw caution to the wind when in sight of friendly forces. The soldier must overcome this tendency and understand that link-up is a very sensitive situation.

If he has made his way to a friendly or neutral country, he uses the following procedures to cross the border and link up with friendly forces on the other side:

1) Occupy a hide site on the near side of the border and send a team out to reconnoitre the potential crossing site.

2) Observe the crossing site for at least 24 hours, depending on the enemy situation.

3) Make a sketch of the site, taking note of terrain, obstacles, guard routines and rotations, and any sensor devices or trip wires.

4) Once the reconnaissance is complete, the team moves to a hide site, briefs the rest of the team and plans to cross the border at night.

BORDER CROSSING TECHNIQUES

Training in border-crossing techniques will focus on the following skills of fieldcraft. Always assume the area is under enemy observation. Move slowly. Do not cause overhead movement of trees, bushes or tall grasses by rubbing against them. Plan every movement and move in segments of the route at a time. Stop, look and listen often. Move during disturbances such as gunfire, explosions, aircraft noise, wind or anything that will distract the enemy's attention or conceal the team's movement.

There are four main techniques for moving across hostile territory. They have been developed and refined by soldiers and snipers for nearly 100 years.

The low crawl – this is used when concealment is extremely limited, when close to the enemy or when occupying a firing position. The soldier keeps his legs together and pushes with toes and pulls with his fingers. If he is armed, he hooks the sling of his rifle between his thumb and index finger and tows it beside him.

The medium crawl – this is used when concealment is limited and the team needs to move faster than the low crawl allows. The soldier lies flat on ground with legs spread and pushes with his legs and uses his elbows to pull himself forward. As with the low crawl, the rifle may be held by its sling or in both hands.

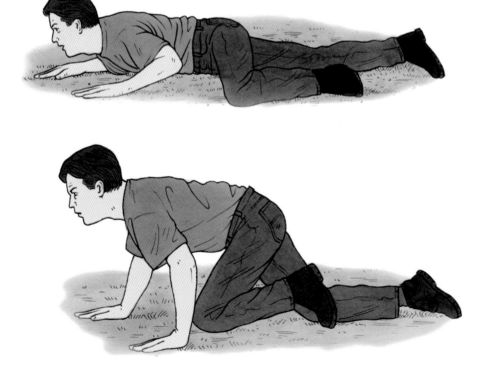

Left: The low crawl (top) is slow but very secure. The survivor/evader literally hugs the ground and moves forward using his knees, toes and forearms to propel himself. The medium crawl (below) is faster and also allows the survivor/evader to scan the terrain – a common mistake is to lower the head and shoulders but keep the bottom sticking up.

Above: Walking or running is ideal in dead ground where the man is concealed. He stays low with his body bent forward. Running is quick but often very noisy, so the survivor/ evader must evaluate if it is safe to employ it.

The high crawl – this is used when concealment is limited but high enough to allow the soldier to raise his body off the ground. He moves on elbows and knees with his body raised off ground and cradles his weapon in his arms.

Walking/running – this is used when there is good concealment, it is not likely the enemy is close, and speed is required. The soldier crouches with body bent forward and knees bent. His weapon is in line with the body with the muzzle pointed down.

OBSTACLES

The border may be demarcated by barbed wire fences or minefields. The barbed wire may be similar to a conventional cattle fence attached to pickets or posts. It may be coils of concertina wire or a combination of both. To cut through a wire fence with stealth, the soldier should cut only the lower strands and leave the top strand in place. This procedure makes it less likely that the enemy will discover the gap. With a tall wire fence, his gap will be at ground level and should be hard to detect if border guards are making a quick visual inspection.

He should cut the wire near a picket. To reduce the noise of a cut, another soldier wraps cloth around the wire and holds it with both hands. He then cuts part of the way through the wire between the other soldier's hands and has him flex the wire until it breaks. If he is a lone evader, he should wrap cloth around the wire near a picket, partially cut the wire, and then bend and break the wire.

To breach an obstacle made of concertina wire, the soldier should cut the wire and stake it back to keep the breach open far enough to allow room to crawl through or under the obstacle. Care should be taken with concertina fences since they are like a spring under tension and if mishandled can produce considerable noise. Concertina wire may also be strung with empty ration or drinks cans that will rattle as the wire springs closed. To speed up crossing concertina wire, boards, doors or grass mats can be laid over the wire to compress it.

If wire cutters are not available, the soldier/evader may be able to crawl under a wire obstacle. To do this he slides, headfirst on his back, pushing forward with his heels. If armed, he should carry his weapon lengthwise on his body and steady it with one hand. To prevent the wire from snagging on his clothes and equipment, he should let it slide along the weapon. He should feel ahead with his free hand to find the next strand of wire and any tripwires or mines.

To cross over a wire obstacle, the soldier stays crouched down low and feels and looks for tripwires and mines. Grasping the first wire strand lightly, he cautiously lifts one leg over the wire. He then lowers his foot to the ground and repeats the same procedure with the other foot. If there is a small group, a speedy way to cross a fence is to have two men stand braced holding the wire near a picket – the third man can climb using the wire as steps and the shoulders of his two companions for support.

MINES

A more serious obstacle for the soldier/evader is a minefield. Mines fall into two categories, anti-tank (AT) and anti-personnel (AP). On a battlefield, AT mines will be laid to block or canalize armoured formations, and since they require the weight of a tank or truck to detonate, will not present a hazard to a man. However, sometimes AP mines are mixed in with AT mines to make manual lifting more hazardous, so all minefields should be treated with respect.

Anti-personnel Mines

AP mines fall into two groups, blast or shrapnel. The latter may be bounding omni-directional or directional. The majority of AP blast mines are the size of a shoe polish tin and pressure-operated, with a mechanical fuzing system initiating a main charge housed in an outer casing. Most use TNT as the main charge, though smaller mines use more powerful explosives such as Tetryl, or mixtures such as Composition B. Plastic casings are used for easy manufacture and most are waterproof. The use of metal for the casing is rare, though wood was used in older designs.

Many modern mines are scatterable, with robust plastic bodies and integral shock-resistant fuzes that enable them to survive drop impact when dispensed from the air. The shock-resistant fuzes also make scatterable mines blast-resistant, giving them substantial protection against explosive mine countermeasures. Some AP blast mines are designed with a minimal metallic content to hamper detection. However, most contain some metal and can be located by metal detectors. Booby-trapping AP blast mines is rare, although electronic versions of some modern mines incorporate an anti-handling device to discourage manual clearance.

Left: With mine markers tucked into his body armour, a Ukrainian soldier works his way forward, searching for mines. He is looking for the prongs of an anti-personnel mine or the slight depression in the ground that shows where an anti-tank mine has been buried.

One of the oldest designs is the (originally wooden) box type, which uses a hinged lid on a rectangular box body. These are sometimes called 'shoe' or 'shoe-box' mines; misnomers derived from the German Schu-minen 42 of the Second World War. Most AP blast mines are now cylindrical, with either a smooth pressure plate bearing on an internal fuze, or a protruding spigot fuze in a central well. To ensure safety during transit, they tend to have a removable fuze or detonator assembly and a mechanical safety device, which must be removed in order to arm them. The use of irregular shapes (such as the Russian PFM-1) is exceptional and confined to scatterable mines with a requirement for compact packaging.

AP blast mines – These are normally surface-laid or buried at depths ranging from 10 to 40mm (0.4–1.5in); at greater depths, the fuze may be too well protected by the soil to operate reliably. The normal laying patterns are either linear, sometimes alternating with AT mines, or in clusters of two to four surrounding an AT mine.

AP blast mines rely primarily on the shock wave produced by high-explosive detonation to cause injury, though a degree of fragmentation is inevitable as the casing and fuze assembly are shattered. The effect is normally localized and unlikely to cause more than one serious casualty per mine, although mines with thick Bakelite casings (like the Russian PMN) do create a more substantial fragmentation hazard. Although the size of charge varies considerably between mines, most are intended to cause serious injury rather than kill. A typical wound will destroy one foot or leg and cause multiple lacerations from casing fragments and surrounding debris.

AP bounding fragmentation mines – This type of mine relies primarily on the projected shrapnel to cause injury. The effective range is affected by the size of charge, height of detonation, thickness of casing and efficiency of fragmentation, or quantity of pre-formed fragments. All produce a horizontal fan of fragments over a complete (360°) circle. AP bounding fragmentation mines generally cause fatal injuries to those nearby, and are capable of inflicting consistently serious

Above: Using a mine prodder, a British Royal Engineer moves carefully through an area that is believed to be mined. The prodder is pushed into the ground at a shallow angle and if it impacts on something solid, the sapper begins to dig around it to ascertain if it is a mine.

wounds at distances between 20 and 100m (66–328ft), depending on the mine. Isolated fragments can be dangerous at even greater distances.

The majority of AP bounding fragmentation mines are about the size of a baked beans can and are tripwire-operated, though several are also capable of pressure or electrical command initiation. The fuze of a bounding mine does not immediately detonate the main charge, it ignites a propellant that projects the mine body into the air; a second fuzing system is then needed to detonate the mine. A mechanical tripwire fuze or electric cable is inherently resistant to the effects of overpressure, and pressure fuzes tend to use prongs rather than pressure plates. These mines are therefore normally unaffected by explosive mine countermeasures, unless the wire is cut by a line charge. Since they are invariably buried, they are normally waterproofed.

TYPICAL MINE SPECIFICATIONS

BOUNDING FRAGMENTATION MINE

Weight:	1–5kg (2.2–11lb)
Diameter:	60–130mm (2.4–5in)
Explosive weight:	100–500g (3.5–18oz)
Operating pressure:	1–25kg (2.2–55lb)
Lethal radius:	10–30m (32–98ft)
Effective range:	20–100m (66–328ft)

STANDARD AP FRAGMENTATION MINE

Weight:	0.5–3kg (1.1–6.6lb)
Diameter:	50–100mm (2–4in)
Explosive weight:	75–200g (2.6–7oz)
Operating pressure:	1–10kg (2.2–22lb)
Lethal radius:	5–20m (16–66ft)
Effective range:	10–30m (32–98ft)

DIRECTIONAL FRAGMENTATION MINE

Weight:	1.5–25kg (3.3–55lb)
Length/diameter:	110–450mm (4–18in)
Explosive weight:	200g–12kg (7oz–26lb)
Operating pressure:	1–10kg (2.2–22lb)
Lethal radius:	10–100m (32–328ft)
Effective range:	30–200m (98–656ft)

Above: A PROM-1 bounding fragmentation AP mine. Bounding AP mines may have pressure prongs, trip wires or both. Three trip wires may be extended from the mine, allowing it to cover a wide area.

**Above: An AP mine
explodes – invisible in
the picture are the
thousands of metal
chunks or crude ball
bearings built into the
mine, which are
scattered as shrapnel
that can kill or cripple.**

The bodies of most AP bounding fragmentation mines are cylindrical, with the protruding fuze assembly mounted in the top surface. Many of these are based on the design of the German 'S-Mines' of the Second World War, though some obsolete types mount the fuze to one side of the mine body. In Vietnam, the generic name for this type of mine was 'Bouncing Betty'. Older mines generally have cast-iron or steel bodies that are shattered to create shrapnel, but most modern designs use preformed fragments, often set into a plastic matrix.

AP fragmentation mines – These tend to be cylindrical and have the protruding fuze assembly mounted centrally in the top surface. Most are mounted on wooden or metal stakes to optimize the range and effect of the shrapnel, hence the alternative name, 'stake mines'. Those based on the Russian POM-Zs use a cylindrical block of TNT (75 or 100g/3 or 3.5oz), but larger charges (up to 410g/14oz) are used in some types. Some of the older stake mines had concrete bodies containing steel fragments; these have all now been superseded by metal-bodied versions. External grooving gives the older mines a 'pineapple' appearance, while more modern versions tend to have a smooth exterior with internal grooving or preformed fragments.

Fuzes sometimes have a safety device, often a second retaining pin, that must be removed in order to arm the mine. The fuzes are mostly removable as separate assemblies, and some mines have several fuzing options. The fuze and detonator assembly are normally fitted into the top of the mine and one or more anchored tripwires attached to the striker retaining pin. The mine is then armed by the removal of a safety device; some incorporate a delay within the fuzing system to allow the setter time to leave the area safely before the mine becomes armed. After this, the mine is initiated when a pin is removed by tension applied to the tripwire. Actuation of the fuze results in the immediate detonation of the main charge.

AP fragmentation mines rely on the shrapnel produced by the shattering of the mine body to cause injury. The effective range is affected by the size of charge, thickness of casing and efficiency of fragmentation, but all produce a fan of fragments over a complete (360º) circle. AP fragmentation mines often cause fatal injuries to those nearby, and are capable of inflicting consistently serious wounds at distances up to 30m (98ft), the typical effective range.

Directional fragmentation mines – These can be either tripwire-operated or electrically command-initiated. If they are command-initiated, the would-be escaper will have been seen and his chances of survival are hugely reduced. The use of plastic explosive is widespread, though some of the larger mines still use TNT as the main charge. Unlike other types of fragmentation mine, the shrapnel in directional mines is normally preformed as ball-bearings or chopped steel rod; this may be set into a resin matrix or arranged between two thin layers of the casing. Directional fragmentation mines are almost always mounted above ground to maximize their range and effect; most are supplied with legs or mounting brackets

BORDER TRIPWIRES

The use of tripwires makes bounding mines well suited to the creation of continuous linear obstacles like border fences and, because they are better concealed than normal stake-mounted AP fragmentation mines, they are ideal for ambushes and the denial of likely assembly areas. Once the fuze assembly is in place, one or more anchored tripwires are attached and the mine is armed by the removal of a safety device. Some incorporate a delay within the fuzing system to allow the setter to leave the area in safety before the mine becomes armed. After this, the mine is initiated by pressure, electrical command or tension applied to the tripwire. Actuation of the fuze results in the mine body being fired into the air by a propellant charge, sometimes after a short delay to allow the victim to step clear. When the mine is well above ground level, typically 0.5 to 1.5m (1.6–5ft), the main charge is detonated by the secondary fuzing system, scattering fragments in all directions.

for fixing to trees. Although generally considered under the heading of AP mines, many of the larger varieties were clearly designed to attack light vehicles or helicopters on approaching or landing.

There are two types of directional fragmentation mine. The 'Claymore' type is rectangular; the shrapnel is normally arranged against a convex front face, with one or two detonator wells moulded into the top surface or back. The second type is round, with a concave front face and a central detonator well. In both cases, the main charge is positioned behind the fragmentation component, across the full width of the mine.

If electrically initiated, the mine may be used with any form of sensor package or electrical switch; when tripwire initiated, a single wire is normally used. A safety device is almost always incorporated into the initiation system. The sizes of directional fragmentation mines vary considerably, and they are often improvised in the field from readily available materials. Larger Claymore types tend to have two detonator wells, while some round varieties have a hole right through the centre, allowing initiators to be inserted from the front or back.

Directional fragmentation mines rely primarily on the projected shrapnel to cause injury. The effective range is affected by the size of charge, quantity of fragmentation and the tightness of the shrapnel pattern. Rectangular Claymore types produce a horizontal fan of fragments (normally over an arc of around 60°)

Below: The generic minefield sign put up in the Falklands to mark Argentine minefields. Since the Italian made mines were constructed from plastic, they will not corrode or rust and will remain a hazard virtually forever.

while round mines create a narrow cone of shrapnel, similar to the spread of pellets from a shotgun. Directional fragmentation mines normally cause fatal injuries to those in direct line nearby, and are capable of inflicting consistently serious wounds up to the quoted effective range.

MINEFIELD EVASION

For the evader or soldier, the good news is that the minefield will probably be marked and fenced. While there are NATO standard signs, the most widely known sign is the skull and crossed bones and the words MINES. A minefield is not an impassable barrier and can be crossed by prodding to locate the mines.

The soldier should first remove his helmet, load-carrying equipment (LCE), watch, rings, belt, identity tags and anything else that may hinder movement or fall off. He leaves his rifle and equipment with another soldier in the team. Taking a wooden stick about 30cm (12in) long, he sharpens one of the ends. In the past, bayonets were used as probes, but it is inadvisable to use a metal probe, as some mines are triggered by magnetic reaction.

The soldier places the unsharpened end of the probe in the palm of one hand with his fingers extended and his thumb holding the probe. He probes every 5cm (2in) across a 1m (3.2ft) front, pushing the probe gently into the ground at an angle less than 45°. He should kneel (or lie down) and feel upward and forward with his free hand to find tripwires and the pressure prongs of anti-personnel mines before starting to probe. The soldier puts just enough pressure on the probe for it to sink it slowly into the ground. If the probe does not go into the ground, he should pick or chip the dirt away with the probe and remove it by hand. He should stop probing when a solid object is touched and remove enough dirt to see what type of mine it is.

He should then mark it and report its exact location to the group leader. There are several ways to mark a mine. How it is marked is not as important as having everyone understand the marking. A common way to mark a mine is to tie a piece of paper, cloth, or engineer tape to a stake and put the stake in the ground by the mine. However, blobs of shaving foam have even been used in an emergency.

Once a footpath has been probed and the mines marked, a security team should cross the minefield to secure the far side. After the far side is secure, the rest of the group should cross.

NATURAL OBSTACLES

National borders are often aligned with rivers and these may present the final obstacle to a home run. Rivers and streams may be shallow or deep, slow- or fast-moving, narrow or wide. Before the soldier tries to cross a river or stream, he must develop a good plan. The first step is to look for a high place from which he can get a good view of the river or stream. From this place, he can look for a place to cross. If there is no high place, he should climb a tree. Good crossing locations include:

- A level stretch where the river breaks into several channels. Two or three narrow channels are usually easier to cross than a wide river.
- A shallow bank or sandbar. If possible, the soldier selects a point upstream from the bank or sandbar so that the current will carry him to it if he loses his footing.
- A course across the river that leads downstream so that he will cross the current at angle of about 45°.

The depth of a fordable river or stream is no deterrent if he can keep his footing. In fact, deep water sometimes runs more slowly and is therefore safer than fast-moving shallow water. He can always dry his clothes later, or if necessary, make a raft to carry his clothing and equipment across the river.

He must not try to swim or wade across a stream or river when the water is at very low temperatures. The swim could be fatal. Instead, he tries to make a raft. He should wade across only if he can be sure that no more than his feet will get wet, and he must dry his feet vigorously as soon as he reaches the other bank.

If necessary, he can safely cross a deep, swift river or rapids. To swim across a deep, swift river, he should swim with the current, never fight it, trying to keep his body horizontal to the water. This will reduce the danger of being pulled under.

WATER HAZARDS

The following areas possess potential hazards; the evader should avoid them, if possible:

- Obstacles on the opposite side of the river that might hinder his travel. He should try to select the spot from which travel will be the safest and easiest.
- A ledge of rocks that crosses the river. This often indicates dangerous rapids or canyons.
- A deep or rapid waterfall or a deep channel. He should never try to ford a stream directly above or even close to such hazards.
- Rocky places. The survivor/evader may sustain serious injuries from slipping on rocks. Usually, submerged rocks are very slippery, making balance extremely difficult. An occasional rock that breaks the current, however, may be helpful.
- An estuary of a river. An estuary is normally wide, has strong currents and is subject to tides. These tides can influence some rivers many kilometres from their mouths. The soldier should go back upstream to an easier crossing site.
- Eddies. An eddy can produce a powerful backward pull downstream of the obstruction causing the eddy and so pull the soldier under the surface.

In fast, shallow rapids, he should lie on his back, feet pointing downstream, finning his hands alongside his hips. This action will increase buoyancy and help him steer away from obstacles. He should keep his feet up to avoid getting them bruised or caught by rocks.

In deep rapids, he should lie on his stomach, head downstream, angling toward the shore whenever he can. He must watch for obstacles and be careful of backwater eddies and converging currents, as they often contain dangerous swirls. Converging currents occur where new watercourses enter the river or where water has been diverted around large obstacles such as small islands.

To ford a swift, treacherous stream, he should adopt the following steps: remove his trousers and shirt to lessen the water's pull. Keep his footwear on to protect his feet and ankles from rocks. It will also provide him with firmer footing.

Tie his trousers and other articles to the top of his rucksack or in a bundle, if he has no pack. This way, if he has to release his equipment, all his articles will be together. It is easier to find one large pack than to find several small items. Carry his pack well up on his shoulders and be sure he can easily remove it, if necessary.

Above: A soldier of the US 2nd Infantry Division crosses a river while undergoing SERE (survival, evasion, resistance and escape) training. He has clipped himself onto the rope with a carabiner, but uses his arms and legs to propel himself across.

Not being able to get a pack off quickly enough can drag down even the strongest swimmers under.

He should find a strong pole about 7.5cm (3in) in diameter and 2–2.5m (6.5–8ft) long to help him ford the stream. He grasps the pole and plants it firmly on the upstream side to break the current. Moving cautiously with each step, he repositions the pole forward a little downstream from its previous position, but still upstream. With the next step, he places his foot below the pole and keeps the pole well slanted so that the force of the current keeps the pole against his shoulder. He should cross the stream so that he will move at a 45° angle to the current.

Once he has made it to safety, the survivor/evader will have a medical examination and be debriefed about his experiences. He will have valuable insights to pass on about survival and evasion as well as conditions inside enemy territory.

OVER THE BORDER

After crossing the border, the soldier (or team) sets up a hide site and tries to locate friendly positions. He should not reveal his presence. Depending on the size of his movement team, two men should observe the potential link-up site with friendly forces until satisfied that the personnel are indeed friendly.

For making contact with the friendly forces during daylight, personnel chosen to make the contact should be unarmed, have no equipment and have positive

RIVER CREATURES

Rivers have other hazards besides fast currents and the consequent risk of drowning. Common sense will tell the evader to avoid confrontations with hippopotami, alligators, crocodiles and other large river creatures. There are, however, a few smaller river creatures with which he should be cautious.

Electric eels (Electrophorus electricus) may reach 2m (6.5ft) in length and 20cm (8in) in diameter, and must be avoided. They are capable of generating up to 500 volts of electricity in certain organs in their body. They use this shock to stun prey and enemies. Normally these eels are only found in the Orinoco and Amazon River systems in South America. They seem to prefer shallow waters that are more highly oxygenated and provide more food. Their upper body is dark grey or black, with a lighter-coloured underbelly.

Piranhas (Serrasalmo species) are another hazard of the Orinoco and Amazon River systems, as well as the Paraguay River Basin, where they are native. These fish vary greatly in size and coloration, but usually have a combination of orange undersides and dark tops. They have white, razor-sharp teeth that are clearly visible. They may be as long as 50cm (20in). The survivor/evader should use great care when crossing waters where they live. Blood attracts them. They are most dangerous in shallow waters during the dry season.

identification readily available. The person who actually makes the link-up should be someone who looks least like the enemy. This can include build, skin coloration and clothing. During the actual approach, only one person makes the contact. The other person provides the security and observes the link-up area from a safe distance. The observer should be far enough away so that he can warn the rest of the movement team if something goes wrong.

The individual making contact should wait until the friendly personnel look in his direction so that he does not surprise them. He stands up from behind cover, with hands overhead and states his nationality. After this, he follows any instructions given him. He avoids answering any tactical questions and does not give any indication that there are other team members – he reveals that there are other personnel with him only after verifying his identity and satisfying himself he has made contact with friendly forces.

Language problems or difficulties confirming identities may arise. The movement team should maintain security, be patient and have a contingency plan. If he is moving to a neutral country, he is surrendering to that power and therefore becomes a detained person.

LINKING UP WITH FRIENDLY PATROLS

If friendly lines are a circular perimeter or an isolated camp, any direction the soldier approaches from will be considered enemy territory. He may not have the

Right: A soldier of the 1st Battalion, The Grenadier Guards works his way cautiously through the jungle in Brunei. The final approach to a friendly border or unit requires patience and caution.

LINK-UP AT THE FEBA/FLOT

If caught between friendly and enemy forces and there is heavy fighting in the area, it may be more advisable for the soldier to hide and let the friendly forces move over him (if they are advancing). If overrun by friendly forces, he may try to link-up from their rear during daylight hours. If overrun by enemy forces, he may move further to the enemy rear, try to move to the forward edge of the battle area (FEBA)/forward line of own troops (FLOT) during a lull in the fighting, or move to another area along the front.

The actual link-up will be done as for link-up during a border crossing. The only difference is that the soldier must be more careful on initial contact. Frontline personnel are more likely to shoot first and ask questions later, especially in areas of heavy fighting. He should be near or behind cover before trying to make contact.

option of moving behind the lines and trying to link up. This move makes the link-up extremely dangerous. One option he has is to place the perimeter under observation and wait for a friendly patrol to move out in his direction, providing a chance to safely reveal himself. He may also occupy a position outside of the perimeter and call out to get the attention of the friendly forces.

The friendly lines must be studied intently before moving towards them. The soldier finds a concealed position that allows him maximum visual coverage of the area. He should try to memorize every terrain feature so that, if necessary, he can infiltrate into friendly positions under the cover of darkness, although trying to infiltrate in darkness is extremely dangerous.

Making contact with combat and reconnaissance patrols should be approached with great caution. He can observe a patrol's route and approach friendly lines at about the same location. Such observation will enable him to avoid mines and booby traps.

Once he has spotted a patrol, he remains in position and, if possible, allows the patrol to move toward him. When the patrol is 25–50m (82–164ft) from his position, he should signal them and call out a greeting that is clearly and unmistakably friendly and recognizable. (In the First Gulf War, one Iraqi soldier who was at college in the United States had been conscripted during a visit to his family and sent to a frontline unit. When he emerged from a bunker to surrender, he wore Bermuda shorts and a Hawaiian shirt – an outfit that was completely unthreatening.)

If he has nothing white, an article of clothing will suffice to draw attention. If the distance is greater than 50m (164ft), a reconnaissance patrol may avoid contact and bypass his position. If the distance is less than 25m (82ft), a patrol member may react instantly by firing a fatal shot. It is crucial at the time of contact that

Below: Waving a white flag and showing that he is unarmed, the survivor/evader makes his presence known to a friendly patrol. They may assume that he is an enemy soldier, so his movements should be slow and deliberate and he should announce clearly who he is and his unit or formation. Quick movements will produce instant reactions in the patrol who may open fire.

there is enough light for the patrol to identify him as friendly. From the perspective of the friendly patrol or friendly personnel occupying a perimeter, he is hostile until they make positive identification.

MIND YOUR LANGUAGE

History is full of tales of soldiers using language, sometimes bad, to establish their nationality. However since English has been widely adopted as a second language around the world even English spoken with a regional accent may not be a guarantee that the figure in the half light or on the fringes of the jungle is friendly.

During the Falklands Campaign of 1982, Argentine Marines who had picked up idiomatic English from watching American films and TV programmes taunted the British soldiers during the night-time fighting around Stanley. These shouts in the darkness in American English produced short-lived rumours that American mercenaries were fighting on the islands.

EXTRACTION TECHNIQUES

Special Forces may have to be extracted following a mission deep inside enemy territory, and many of the requirements for this type of operation are relevant for an evader. Sometimes long-range communications may have been established between friendly forces and the evader, and an extraction team sent to get him out. The terrain is important in choosing the point of extraction – for example, whether or not the extraction site offers good cover from enemy direct-fire weapons and positions from which the extracting force can suppress the enemy. Tidal conditions and Pick-up Zone (PZ) size must be considered. Unlikely locations such as swamps, jungles or mountain areas are often used for extraction, as they are usually the least populated by enemy soldiers. Specially trained air and naval crews, using the latest extraction devices, make such terrain useable.

During the Vietnam War, helicopters flying "Dust Offs" – casualty evacuation missions – could lower a hinged seat through the jungle canopy. The "Jungle Penetrator" was compact enough to get through the canopy, and the wounded soldier was then strapped to the hinged seat and winched up to the hovering helicopter. It was an invaluable aid for speedy evacuation, obviating the need to clear an LZ. The only problem was with a dog handler and his charge. They worked as a close knit team and if man or dog was wounded the SOPs were that they were to be evacuated together – this was difficult if all that was available was a Jungle Penetrator.

Extraction is best conducted without enemy pressure. However, such pressure could develop during the operation. Detailed plans are made for emergency or contingency extractions forced by the enemy as well as clandestine extractions not under enemy pressure. If under pressure, units will have to use planned fire support to suppress enemy weapons. At the beginning of the extraction, with security posted to provide early warning, the unit may start to thin out the same as with a

Above: Flares designed
to spoof heat-seeking
surface-to-air missiles
curve away from a
MH-53J Pave Low
helicopter. These US Air
Force helicopters are
used to insert special
forces and are equipped
with sophisticated
navigation aids like
forward-looking infrared
radar, GPS and terrain
avoidance radar.

night withdrawal. Ground security may be relied on until the last unit withdraws under cover of suppressive fires.

If enemy contact is made during an extraction, the commander must decide whether to reinsert units or break contact and move to another extraction point. Fire support and suppression are important. The Special Forces unit may have special weapons systems or equipment to aid in the extraction. Shoulder-fired anti-aircraft missiles, for example, may be used to defend against enemy aircraft threatening the extraction.

Extraction by air or water is preferred when the resources are available and their use will not endanger the mission. Other factors that favour their use are when:
• Long distances must be covered.
• Time of return is essential.
• The enemy does not have air and naval superiority.
• Heavily populated hostile areas block land movement.
• Special Forces may be burdened with prisoners of war, casualties or carrying critical items of equipment.

If an overland exfiltration is necessary, stealth is the key requirement. This method of extraction is favoured when:

- The enemy has air superiority.
- The enemy is able to prohibit air or water extraction.
- The distance to friendly lines is short.
- The terrain provides cover and concealment (for movement on foot) and limits enemy mobile units.

LAND EXFILTRATION – THE HARD WAY

On 24 December 1942, during operations in North Africa, Lieutenant Bill Fraser of the Special Air Service (SAS) and his patrol were tasked with attacking an Axis airfield near a feature known as 'Marble Arch', but on the night they found no targets. A confusion about the RV with the Long Range Desert Group patrol which was to pick them up resulted in Fraser and his patrol waiting for a week in the desert. With their water low, Fraser, the Sergeants DuVivier and Tait and two other soldiers, started walking, but by now they were reported missing. At one point, they had only about 300ml (0.5 pints) of water per man, and DuVivier recalled that they sucked pebbles to keep their saliva going. After a 322km (200-mile) march over two weeks, during which they hijacked an Italian truck and then a German staff car, they reached Allied lines at Kabrit.

Below: An SAS Jeep in Libya in 1942 showing the modifications and fuel and water stowage and armament, including twin Vickers K guns and a Browning .50 cal (12.7mm) machine gun.

Multiple routes of exfiltration may be used to prevent destruction of the force if soldiers or units are detected. Captured enemy vehicles and equipment may also be used to assist in the exfiltration. Depending on circumstances, exfiltration may take place in one body or in small groups. Exfiltrating in small groups avoids the time delay of assembly. The exfiltrating force should be lightly equipped and not burdened with captured personnel or material, and ideally the exfiltration route passes through an area occupied by friendly civilians or guerrilla forces who can assist the movement. Areas along exfiltration routes should not be heavily inhabited.

Below: US Navy aircrew Robert Wetzel and Jeffrey Zaun, who were shot down and captured in Iraq during the Gulf War on January 18, 1991. Zaun was interviewed on video by the Iraqis as a propaganda ploy. Both Wetzel and Zaun were released on March 3, 1991 – up to that point the US military did not know if Wetzel was alive.

DEBRIEF

The opportunity to analyze the experiences of service personnel who have been captured, interrogated and detained in a conflict, or evaded and escaped is uniquely valuable. Training and equipment evaluation exercises can be made very intense, but they can never replicate the pressure and unpredictability of 'the real thing'. Specialists and experts will want to know what items of equipment were useful and therefore merit further development, and those that were of marginal value.

Intelligence officers will want to know about hostile interrogation techniques and also about what information the enemy was seeking. They will be interested to know what the ex-prisoner or evader saw or heard, either about other prisoners or enemy equipment or operational techniques. Interesting as this is to both soldier and intelligence officer, the escaper or evader should remember that he is not engaged in an espionage operation, and if he is caught gathering intelligence while dressed in civilian clothes, he could be in deep trouble. His aim is to get home in one piece.

The survivor/evader is valuable, able to speak with the authority of personal experience. He will be an inspiration for others at risk of capture in current or future operations, and a caution for those who might think 'it won't happen to me'.

Depending on how long a serviceman has been held captive, there will also be a process of reintegration. This will begin with a medical check – service personnel tend to be fit, but diseases or infections can be picked up on the run or inside a prison camp or cell. The tropics can harbour a variety of medical problems, from fungal infections to long-lasting internal disorders that are incurable.

Psychologial Effects

Even if the physical condition of the soldier is sound, it can be harder to evaluate the psychological effects of his experience. Survivors may suffer from deep feelings of anxiety or guilt, knowing that they lived and others died within the unit or camp. To survive, some men may have had to sacrifice friends and principles or watch as this happened around them. These feelings of guilt and shame may affect the rest of their lives, hampering their ability to live a fulfilled and happy life.

Assuming that he is physically and psychologically sound, the ex-prisoner may need to be brought up to date with current international and domestic affairs. Former US prisoners from North Vietnam who knew nothing of developments in the space race with the USSR, or the change of presidents in the USA, were given a condensed history of the events that had happened while they were in isolation.

Spouses and children may also require support. After the Second World War, there was little public acceptance of Post Traumatic Stress Disorder (PTSD). Some writers in women's magazines in the USA wrote confidently that returning soldiers would settle down quickly in the secure environment of a happy home with a loving wife. In reality, many wives struggled alone to cope with men who were deeply scarred and damaged. Wives spoke of men tortured by nightmares, or who were unable to sleep unless they had a handgun or combat knife within reach.

Counselling and support is invaluable, but a very delicate operation. Some people may have buried memories so deeply that they have almost forgotten them; bringing them to the surface and encouraging discussion may be traumatic.

For some men and women, a strong religious faith or deeply held political creed, as well as the love of a spouse and children, will provide support both during and after survival or capture. For them, there is a happy ending.

ESCAPE FROM YUGOSLAVIA

In the late 20th century, the air war over former Yugoslavia produced two memorable combat search-and-rescue operations. One attracted considerable publicity, while the other remains wrapped in secrecy. Both, however, were triumphs of the individual and the rescue team.

On 2 June 1995, US Air Force Captain Scott O'Grady (29) was shot down by a surface-to-air missile south of the Bosnian city of Banja Luka. An F-16 pilot stationed in Aviano, Italy, O'Grady was part of the NATO group enforcing the no-fly zone over the former Yugoslavia. For six days, O'Grady managed to evade capture by Bosnian Serb forces, camouflaging himself in dirt and leaves, drinking rainwater or sucking on his own sodden socks, and eating the occasional ant.

'At the most,' said O'Grady 'I ate 12 ants. They're sour, like a lemon, and crunchy. My primary concern when I was out there wasn't to eat but to drink water. I was very dehydrated and was very concerned about water intake because you will die from dehydration much quicker than you will from any type of malnutrition. I had a couple of packages of water in my survival pack and rainwater, and at the very end, when I didn't have anything, I drank the sweat out of my socks.'

Then, in a daring rescue on the morning of 8 June, he was picked up by US Marines from the 24th Marine Expeditionary Unit (Special Operations Capable) embarked on USS *Kearsarge* (LHD 3), covered by NATO air forces to suppress the anti-air threat.

Officers running the operation were hoping to launch a night rescue to take advantage of the military's night-vision technology. But when

Above: Captain Scott O'Grady during the press conference following his evasion and extraction from Bosnia in 1995. O'Grady survived for six days before his radio signal was picked up.

O'Grady's signal was received – just hours before dawn – the decision had to be made whether to wait another 18 hours until nightfall or attempt a daylight extraction. Two hours and five minutes after receiving O'Grady's signal that gave his call sign 'This is Basher 5-2', the helicopters were inbound and authenticating who he was by asking him his high school nickname. With a good identification, they moved in, requested that he 'pop smoke' (throw a smoke grenade) and then landed and picked him up.

The Marine Corps rescue team was on the ground in just a little over two minutes, and had the downed pilot aboard a helicopter and headed for safety. The whole operation from the authentication to the pick-up was about 10 minutes.

Unfortunately, they were not yet out of danger. 'We hit the tanker and when we came back up to Magic frequency the helicopters were about 13 miles from "feet wet" [USS *Kearsarge* (LHD 3)]' recalled the USAF fighter pilot who had located O'Grady. '[I] heard the escort helicopter, [...] say, "Bud, impacts underneath you. SAMS IN THE AIR! SAMS IN THE AIR!" [...] Luckily, they missed, although they took some small arms fire – apparently the gunner from [the escort helicopter] silenced that.'

Interviewed in November 2000 by the Pittsburgh, Pa. *Post-Gazette*, O'Grady said modestly, 'There are individuals who've gone through 10 times worse than I ever did, who came home to nothing, no recognition at all. In fact, some of them were ridiculed and spat on. Some of the downed pilots in North Vietnam who ended up in the Hanoi Hilton for more than seven years and the horrific things they went through. You keep in perspective individuals like Nick Rowe, who was in prisoner camps in Vietnam for five years. That man went through hell for five years. I was on a little camping trip for six days, just trying to hide from people. That's why I dedicated my book [*Return with Honor*] to them, because I thought about them and they gave me inspiration when I was struggling. I thought about how tough I was having it, but I realized the worst day I was having was a lot better than their best day being a prisoner.'

O'Grady, who has now retired from the United States Air Force, was awarded a Bronze Star, a Purple Heart and an Air Force Commendation Medal for meritorious service.

On Saturday 27 March 1999, a US Air Force F-117A Nighthawk fighter-bomber went down near Belgrade, becoming the first NATO aircraft lost during NATO strikes against Yugoslavia to prevent Serbian atrocities in Kosovo. The F-117A (82-0806/HO) was, according to the Serbs, shot down by a SA-6 missile near Budjanovci about 45km (30 miles) west of Belgrade. However, it may have come down through technical failure.

The pilot ejected and was rescued hours later by a NATO search-and-rescue team and flown back to Aviano Air Base, where he received medical attention.

The crash of the aircraft was notable because the Nighthawk was the world's first operational aircraft designed to exploit low-observable stealth technology. A precision-strike aircraft, it was created to penetrate high-threat airspace and employ laser-guided weapons against critical targets. Although the plane was destroyed, US combat search-and-rescue units were able to enter Yugoslavia and rescue the American pilot within six hours of the crash. The Pentagon refused to provide details of the pilot rescue mission, which was led by a joint US Special Forces unit. 'There may be times when we have to rescue pilots and the less said, the better for the safety of the pilots,' said a Pentagon spokesman.

The pilot, who was not publicly identified, was reported in 'good condition' and 'was relieved to be out of Yugoslavia and back at base,' he said.

Bibliography

AFM 64-5. *Survival.* Boulder, Colorado: Paladin Press, 1979.

Dach Bern, von, Major H. *Total Resistance.* Boulder, Colorado: Panther Publications, 1965.

Fowler, William. *Operation Barras: the SAS Rescue Mission.* Sierra Leone 2000. London: Weidenfeld & Nicolson, 2004.

—SAS Behind Enemy Lines. London: HarperCollins, 1997.

FM7-93. *Long Range Surveillance Unit Operations.* USA: HQ Department of the Army, 1995.

FM21-76. *Survival, Evasion and Escape.* USA: HQ Department of the Army, 1969.

FM21-77. *Escape and Evasion.* USA: HQ Department of the Army, 1958.

Mears, Ray. *Essential Bushcraft.* London: Hodder & Stoughton, 2002.

Canadian Government. *Never Say Die: the Canadian Air Force Survival Manual.* Boulder, Colorado: Paladin Press, 1982.

Reid, Pat, MBE, MC. *Prisoner of War.* London: Hamlyn, 1984.

Toliver, Raymond. *The Interrogator.* Fallbrook, USA: Aero Publishers, 1978.

Wiseman, John. *SAS Survival Handbook.* London: HarperCollins, 1986.

Websites

Code of Conduct for the Armed Forces of the United States:
http://usmilitary.about.com/library/weekly/aa032403a.htm

Survival Skills: http://dnausers.d-n-a.net/prepared/skills.html

The Great Escape: Rob Davis: http://www.elsham.pwp.blueyonder.co.uk/gt_esc/

The Smoking Gun Archive: http://www.thesmokinggun.com

USAF Air Rescue Service: http://www.wpafb.af.mil/museum/history/rescue/res16.htm

Wilderness Survival: http://www.wilderness-survival.net

Explanation Guide: http://explanation-guide.info/meaning

Picture Credits

Index